Enter Whining

Enter Whining

Fran Drescher

ReganBooks

An Imprint of HarperCollins*Publishers*

FIRST EDITION

Designed by Nancy Singer

Jacket credits: *photography:* Alberto Tolot; *makeup:* Carol Shaw for Lorac; *hair:* Enzo Angileri for Cloutier; *styling:* Phillip Bloch for Cloutier; *dress:* Giorgio Armani; *jewelry:* Van Cleef & Arpels.

ISBN 0-06-039155-3

96 97 98 99 00 ❖/RRD 10 9 8 7 6 5 4 3 2 1

To my mother, my father, Elaine, and my high school sweetheart and husband, Peter, for without the love and devotion of each of them, none of this could have been possible

Acknowledgments

There were those who were particularly helpful in the long, arduous, and often tedious process of putting together as well as promoting this book. I would like to thank from the bottom of my heart these unsung heroes:

Howie Preiser
Cari Ross
David Pecker
TriStar Television
CBS Inc.
Regan Books/HarperCollins

And a special thanks to Jeff Sagansky for believing in me.

Contents

Enter Whining

Chapter 1

In the Beginning

My assistant informed me that I was being summoned by the president of the company, my boss—a king among kings *and* a barracuda. But how else do you get to the top at his age? I opened the door and saw him: a snake in Armani. "Come to Daddy," he said in anything but a fatherly tone, and I obeyed as he pulled off his crocodile belt and cracked it against his massive mahogany desk. How could I have let myself get into this situation, and why couldn't I bring myself to stop? But he was my addiction and I, his slave. As I stood before him, my thighs quivered and my nipples hardened as he slowly unbuttoned my blouse with one hand and began to reach under my skirt, sliding up between my legs with the other . . . NOT!!

Sorry, those things totally don't happen to me, but Jackie

Collins once said on a talk show that if she didn't grab her reader in the very first paragraph, she was screwed. Meanwhile, I'm quoting Jackie Collins, so who's screwed—her or me?

Actually, I've been with the same man since I was fifteen, my best friend and soul mate, Peter Jacobson. I often say that I can recall a time when Peter had *no* hairs on his chest, and now the hairs on his chest are *gray*. He's thrilled when I tell people that.

Peter at fifteen in his David Cassidy layer cut.

We both remember the first moment we laid eyes on each other. I was walking up and he was walking down the stairwell in Hillcrest High, Jamaica, Queens. Me with my Farrah Fawcett wings and eight-inch Goody Two–shoes, him with his dry-cleaned blue jeans and David Cassidy layer cut. Peter later admitted he thought I was the most beautiful girl he had ever seen, and then I spoke . . . who knew the combo would intrigue him even more, but it did. "You gotta face out of *Vogue* and a voice outta Selma Diamond," he often quips. Well, whatever turns ya on!

We became instant best friends. He used to walk by my house pretending he just happened to be in the neighborhood, and he would linger in front of my apartment building, hoping I'd come out. The funny thing is, he wasn't in front of

Me in high school.

my building at all, and that's why I never came out. He was two houses down and lucky nobody called the police on him.

A lot of people ask what we attribute our seventeen-year marriage to. Screaming! We fight, we yell, and we sometimes hit rock bot-

Peter annoying me in Pisa.

tom just like everyone else, but we both want our marriage to work. So we don't hesitate to seek therapy when we have problems. A good double session with the shrink clears a lot of shit. I think the one thing that Peter and I enjoy most is laughing. A good laugh till you cry. We used to get thrown out of more high school classes because we couldn't stop

laughing. The teachers wouldn't let us sit together because of it, but something would strike one of us as funny and the other would just instinctively know it and glance over, and before you knew it, we were kicked out of class again. We became inseparable.

We even worked together, except for my brief stint as head chicken fryer at the Chicken Jamboree. I used to bring tons of chicken and sweet potato pies home for Pete to eat, except I never cooked the chicken long enough, so it was raw in the middle and the pie was always half-frozen. I couldn't

Peter annoying me in Lake Como.

Peter and I at sixteen, rehearsing for a high school play.

master the techniques. So I decided to leave my career in poultry and moved on to become cashier at the Main St. Movies, where Peter was already usher. Again, we constantly got in trouble for laughing.

In fact, once fifty dollars was missing, and they thought Peter and I were in cahoots. How dare they! We marched ourselves into the main office to clear our good names. Finally, they believed us, but we never felt comfortable working there again. I don't know, maybe I should have stuck with my career at the Chicken Jamboree. Peter quit and decided to try his skills at Baskin-Robbins, but he was fired because he was too creative. He used to take the straws out of the wrappers to put them in the whipped cream of an ice cream soda to give it a little style. Some panache. Something to look at. Well, he was canned. It was actually quite traumatic for him. "What did I do? I sold more than any other salesman." But he just packed up his scooper and never looked back.

My husband will be the first to tell you that he comes from a weird family. A Jewish father, a Catholic mother who had a Jewish mother, and both of them converted to Unitarianism, then moved to a practically Hasidic neighborhood. Needless to say, he had a hard time fitting in, but I think he found solace in my family. We were loud and demonstrative.

Peter used to get a kick out of going out to eat with my family. My father took on the accent of whatever nationality of food we were having. Peter used to sit there with his mouth open. My father thought he would be better understood if he were Mr. Lee at the Chinese restaurant or a Mafia don at Stella D'Oro's Italian trattoria. It was pretty scary.

My parents, Morty and Sylvia, treated Peter as their own. Once, during a storm, my mother got an urge for an ice cream sundae with chocolate sauce, whipped cream, and wet nuts. Oh, she was hinting and hoping that someone would run out during the storm. Peter finally got the hint as my mother practically pushed him out the door. A half hour passed and half-drenched Peter came back with the sundae. Oh, my mother was all atwitter.

"Here it is, Ma. Chocolate ice cream, chocolate sauce, whipped cream, and nuts. Enjoy." My mother's face dropped. "What's wrong?"

"Oh, nothing, it's delicious," she said, as if she had just found out that Kathie Lee had left Regis.

"No, really. What's wrong?" Peter asked.

"Well, if you must know, the nuts." Huh? "I wanted *wet* nuts."

"Oh, I'm sorry," Peter told her. She stared at him with her best starving-mother look. "You don't want me to go back and get the wet ones, do ya?"

"Would ya? I mean, I just can't enjoy it otherwise." He braved the storm so my mother the kishkila (someone who really enjoys their food) would enjoy, and she did, and he still tells the story today.

He relishes making my mother laugh. She once had to stop traffic in the middle of Kissena Boulevard because he'd imitated her and she'd gotten so hysterical that she'd doubled over and started to pee in her pants. She couldn't move. She just loves it when Peter makes fun of her. As I'm writing this, she's telling Peter how she's too nervous to eat before she flies while she's sending my father to get her the corn muffins because she didn't like the cranberry so much. Peter loves my parents and treats them as if they're his own. There's nothing he wouldn't do for them or vice versa.

Now, I come from a very humble background. I was born in New York City, well, actually Queens, well, actually Flushing, and honey, it's a world away from Manhattan. When I was a young child my dad worked two jobs to support us, but when he got home he always made sure he kissed me and my sister, Nadine, good night, even if we were fast asleep. We felt his love. And my mother, the most loving, happy person I'll ever have the privilege of knowing, created an adoring, wonderful, and safe environment in which we kids were able to blossom. They always said, "We don't have a lot of money, but we're very rich anyway." And we were.

I wonder if I was nasal then?

My first performance.

Can you believe those
bangs? What was my
mother thinking?

Me at fourteen going on twenty-two, with
braces. I hadn't even graduated
from junior high yet.

My first attempt at
glamour.

Early years at the bungalow colony.

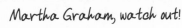

Martha Graham, watch out!

Me and my sister at the
Great Wall of China. (You know, the
restaurant on Queens Boulevard.)

Yetta's hair was
called the pineapple. Only in Queens
would they name a hairdo after fruit.

The Doublemint twin rejects.

My bedroom and my parents' shared a common wall, and over the years I recall so much laughter coming from the other side of that wall. It was music to my ears as I'd lie in bed and stifle conta-

Oy!

gious giggles. I like to regard them as Hansel and Gretel because they've never been spoiled or jaded by life but take genuine pleasure in the simplest things. A happy family, good health, an ice cream sundae with wet nuts, and a two-dollar movie at the multiplex pretty much answers all their prayers, especially if they can sneak into another feature.

While shoving myself into my Sergio Valente jeans for school one morning I heard Harry Harrison, a local deejay, announcing that girls between the ages of thirteen and seventeen should send in a fifteen-dollar check or money order, along with an entrance application, to compete in the Miss New York Teenager pageant. Not what you'd call a terribly discriminating contest—I mean, anyone with fifteen bucks and carfare to Manhattan got in—but I saw this as my ticket to stardom and quickly sent in the money. I

*Ya like the pants?
In a strong wind, I can
take off.*

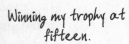

Winning my trophy at fifteen.

Miss New York Teenager—okay, first runner-up.

remember finding the perfect dress at Macy's. Even back then I realized the necessity of looking wholesome, so on the day of the contest I tried my best to look as "white bread" (the industry term for Midwestern) as possible and wore a long bone-satin dress with a soft shoulder ruffle (very Mary Ann Mobley), a tasteful pair of two-inch pumps (ya know, stewardess shoes), and three coats of royal blue mascara (whoopsie). Well, honey, you can take the girl out of Flushing . . .

The contestants were all primping backstage. You could asphyxiate yourself on the hair-spray fumes. Thank God there wasn't a talent competition, because none of us could do anything, but there was the oh-so-important question and answer portion. One contestant told the judge her hobby was sewing, to which the judge asked what it was she liked to sew. And in her authentic Brooklynese she responded, "Uh, rips and

Tenth grade: my first
high school production.

The high school play,
"Black Comedy."

Peter and me in
"Grease."

tears . . ." Hello? Meanwhile, she won, but I placed as first runner-up and left with a fifteen-dollar trophy in my hand. Well, at least I broke even. Today the trophy sits on my vanity in the bedroom set of *The Nanny,* but then I felt like such a loser. I couldn't believe I'd lost to the rips-and-tears chick, but my mom explained, "Fran, placing first runner-up is not bein' a loser, you're a winner . . . it's the three hundred other girls *without* trophies who are the losers!" Ma always had a way of making me feel better with what we on *The Nanny* call simple Queens logic. She's right, I thought, and proceeded to follow through with my plan to use my title as a door opener. Each day after school I would dial talent agencies and introduce myself with my new title: "Hello, my name is Fran Drescher and I'm the *winner* of the Miss New York Teenager pageant!" So I exaggerated a little, sue me. Meanwhile, I got myself an agent.

My first shot. Notice the subtle shirt with the monkeys?

I was going for the natural look ... with a little bit of Lily Munster.

Pippi Drescher. Trying to look ingenue and cute with my Monet earrings.

The natural look.
I could do bodily harm with that mascara.

Chapter 2

So You Wanna
Be a Star?

Mom and Dad were very supportive of Peter and me becoming
actors, as long as we had something to fall back on. But what?
One day, while we were looking in the paper, our prayers were
answered: the Ultissima Beauty Institute. For one thousand
hours you, too, could be the Vidal and Beverly Sassoon of
Flushing (oy, talk about dating oneself). Ladies would come off
the street for two-dollar haircuts. I was pretty good at cuts, but
Peter's specialty was the bouffants and making women cry...

I'll never forget the time Peter and I were streaking my sister's long, ash-blond hair with light blond and proudly
demonstrating the new "weaving" technique we had just
learned in beauty school, when my sister muttered, "Gee, it's
amazing that all the hair is in the tinfoil and yet it's going to

The night Peter and I went to see "Jaws." It took years to get me back in the ocean again.

still have dark streaks." At which point Peter and I looked at each other, like the amateurs that we were, in complete horror and panic, followed by uncontrollable, hysterical laughter. There my poor sister sat, half her head placed in peroxide and tinfoil while the other half remained a dark ash. Well, it was kind of a streak job, except there were only two streaks, one on the left side and one on the right. Oy. I always liked cutting hair the best, anyway.

During those thousand hours of teasing, dyeing, and destroying people's hair, Peter and I went on countless auditions, everything from Crystal Light to Clearasil. We'd pick up the odd print ad or commercial (for some reason, I never spoke in my commercials), but unfortunately, our career in coiffure was looking better and better. Then one day the phone rang. Finally my big break had arrived. I was gonna be doing a film with Gary Busey. All right, he was the star and I was an extra, but remember, there are no small parts, just small salaries.

As it turned out, the young assistant director who was in charge of the extras kinda liked me, so I managed to be an extra in almost every scene in that movie. I was a shopper in a New York street scene, I was a stewardess at the airport—it didn't matter where the movie went, in the background was an eighteen-year-old brunette with stars in her overly made-up eyes. Well, one day early in the shoot I was to play an upscale, sophisticated shopper in Manhattan, along with eight hundred other sophisticated shoppers. Now, as an extra you're expected to supply your own wardrobe, so I showed up in a maroon wrap coat with fur collar (my grandfather was a furrier; he's since died, and I've given up fur completely), matching maroon fedora hat complete with a huge feather plume (hey, it was my debut, I wanted to look nice, plus I wanted my parents to be able to find me in the crowd), and was promptly given my shopping-bag prop by my faithful friend, the adoring assistant director. There I stood on my start mark waiting to hear the "action" word, at which point I began my oh-so-natural, oh-so-realistic stroll down the street, swinging my shopping bag and occasionally glancing over at the shop windows. Boy, I'm really acting now, when suddenly, and purely by accident, I lost my grip on my shopping bag and it slipped out of my hand and onto the street.

In split seconds it ran through my head that the shot wouldn't match all the other takes and that I should probably let them know I'd blown the take, because if I didn't, they'd trace the mistake back to me and I'd never work in this town again. So from a hundred yards away, I began to flail my arms, trying desperately to get the attention of that hardly visible clump known as the director, cameraman, and star, when suddenly, finally, somebody spotted me (the nutcase waving her arms and jumping up and down like a banshee), but no response, so I just yelled "CUT!" For all you aspiring talents out there, don't do that! Everything stopped, all eight hundred shoppers, two hundred crew members, the director, and the star, Gary Busey. Oh, I thought, they are going to be so relieved that I alerted them to this unexpected fly in the ointment, when from out of the masses one red face began to come into focus as it ran toward me. Who else? None other than my admirer, the assistant director, who by now was beginning to break into a sweat, and said to me, with the controlled patience that only love can muster, "What's the problem?"

"Oh, well, ya see, I dropped my shopping bag, and I knew it wouldn't match," I answered with Girl Scout enthusiasm, to which this sweet young man responded, through gritted teeth,

Fran Drescher, country-music legend.

"If that happens again, just pick up the bag and keep moving, okay? You're just a blur in the background." He stormed off. Well, aren't we a little miffed, I thought to myself. As I prepared for the next take, I just chalked the whole thing off to sloppy filmmaking.

It was about one year and a million auditions later that I found myself auditioning for a McDonald's commercial. It was a McNightmare. They wanted either a girl or a boy to lip-sync to some hamburger song while dancing and playing the piano. Here's the catch: You'll also be wearing a giant, rubber moon head, so nobody will know it's you. What did I care? But the really humiliating thing was that when you auditioned, they didn't have the lovely aforementioned moon head, so instead you wore an A & P grocery bag on your head. There I was, dancing around like some idiot with this paper bag on my head, when suddenly I knocked into the wall and practically passed out. Sometimes I think the advertising agency has you do this so they can take home the audition tape and have a good laugh with the family.

Well, I finally landed my first speaking part in a movie, *Saturday Night Fever*. Oh, my God, I'm workin' with a sweathog, the gorgeous one, Vinnie Barbarino! We shot the scene at the 2001 Disco in Brooklyn. The streets were crowded with spectators, but the set remained closed off to everyone except those few lucky enough to be part of the movie. Well, when my dad, who at the time was working in Brooklyn, came by on his lunch break to see my scene, the security guard quickly told him it was a closed set. When my dad informed the guard that he was the star's father (mind you, I had five lines), the guard quickly opened the gate and said, "Right this way, Mr. Travolta." Of course, Morty, thrilled by the identity mix-up, without missing a beat and without flinching a muscle, continued to enter.

Finally it was time to shoot my scene. John seemed to be very down and depressed, and unable to go on with the shoot. My mazel (luck), the scene he wanted to skip was mine. Now there were plenty of people trying to coax him into working some more that afternoon, but I guess the grueling schedule, coupled with the recent death of his girl-friend, was more than he could bear. "You wanna steak, John?" one guy offered. "Maybe he needs a cold drink," said another, but like watching a Greek tragedy, I saw Travolta get cemented into his lump-like position in a corner as my part was going down the drain. Okay, enough's enough! I thought, and marched my way over to John to try to salvage what was fast becoming a disaster—MINE!

A family vacation in Puerto Rico. I cut that dress down and wore it in "Saturday Night Fever."

"Ya know, John, maybe I shouldn't be saying this, but you're a trouper. Whatever happened to 'let's go on with the show'? So what if *you're* tired? So what if *you're* run-down?

Maybe they *will* have to check you in to a hospital for exhaustion in the end, but right now I expect you to act like the star that you are, and finish the scene, then we can all go home!"

Did that just come out of me? Am I crazy? Am I fired? Am I nauseous! He looked at me, oy. He stood up, double oy, and finally he spoke. "Thanks, I needed that, come on, let's dance."

John Travolta grabbed my hand, pulled me onto the lighted disco floor, and began to lead me like no man has ever led me before or since. Hoo-ha! I mean, I didn't even know one single step, but it didn't matter because he holds you so tight and moves you, pushing and pulling, twirling, throwing and catching. Whoo, I'm getting a little overheated here! You become more like a juggler's balls than anything. Like a film-star heroine I thought, I'm here for you, John, as he seemed to regain his strength by feeding off mine. We shot the scene, and it remained in the final cut as the prelude to his famous dance solo. I uttered my first screen words, "Are you as good in bed as you are on the dance floor?" Hey, it wasn't Shakespeare, but I got to grab his tushy (completely my own idea) as we crossed out onto the lit platform of the 2001 club; I looked up at him, a gorgeous hunk of superstar who didn't can my ass, and I have adored him ever since.

But it was an audition on Yom Kippur (the high holy day) for the movie *American Hot Wax* (costarring Jay Leno) that turned out to be my first big break. I was so nervous I thought a good icebreaker would be to talk about corn dood-ies and how they appear in your doody after ingesting too much corn. Hey, at nineteen, toilet humor was hysterical. The director, Floyd Mutrux, seemed to laugh at everything I said. I thought to myself, Why of all days did this audition have to be on Yom Kippur? Watch, I'll get the part, but God will strike me dead. Well, I got the part *and* lived! California here we come!

Me right before I grabbed his tush.

Peter and I drove from the airport, gazing at all the palm trees that lined the streets and feeling like Ellie May and Jethro, but we didn't stop in Beverly Hills (swimmin' pools and movie stars). No, we drove right to the Queens of L.A., the San Fernando Valley. Home to the Sherman Oaks Galleria, Orange Julius, and the Swedish Smorgasbord Dinner Theater. And they say there's no culture in L.A.

"American Hot Wax," with Jay Leno.

Chapter 3

Life in L.A.

We opened the door to our new one-bedroom apartment. It was a study in orange and green plaid, with Danish, modern-looking furniture and lime-green shag carpeting. It was as if we were moving into the Barbie

Our first apartment. Gorgeous, huh? That chair is genuine Naugahyde.

Dream House. If it had only been 1962, it would've been spectacular. Now, since we were only scheduled to stay for a couple of months, we rented everything. Believe it or not, there is actually a place that rents pot holders. Suddenly Peter screamed, "Babe, look, we have a terrace. A three-foot cement box, complete with a dead avocado pit in a jelly jar." Oh, this is nice, we have an outdoor environment.

Peter and me doing TV commercials. Aren't we wholesome?

As Peter looked over the edge of our terrace, he gasped. "Oh, my God, look!" I ran over, and there it was, every Flushing couple's Mecca. The pool. We took a deep breath. As chlorine filled our nostrils, we gazed over the two hundred or so plastic beige and orange chaise lounges circling the sacred watering hole like the June Taylor dancers. Then we noticed what looked like a small bubbling cauldron filled with people. The Jacuzzi. Who could believe that Fran and Peter from Kissena Boulevard are

When we first moved to L.A.

gonna be Jacuzzi-ing? Of course, we didn't picture ourselves shoved in there with thirty other renters all fighting over the six air jets.

Well, once we unpacked, the first order of business was a little decorating. A couple of philodendron plants, some nice black-velvet towels, on which I sewed some lime green pompoms, ya know, to match the carpet, and a trip to Bargain Circus, a store where everything is less than five dollars, completed the look. Watch out, Martha Stewart. We were so proud, we used to drag up all the neighbors to show them what we had done with the place. Peter even bought a rake for the shag carpeting. He used to make designs in the rug with it for special occasions. Hey, we were only nineteen.

We were twenty and took our designer jeans very seriously.

One day, to upgrade the terrace, we went all out and bought AstroTurf and a five-inch hibachi. But I'll tell ya, we had some great times in that apartment. We used to hang out with then unknown actors Dennis Quaid, David Caruso, and Rosanna Arquette, and I'd cook up some real diet specials. Thick rib steaks smoth-

Me with David Caruso. I had just cut his hair.

ered in onions. Spaghetti and meatballs. Pineapple rice with shrimp. Chicken stuffed with Rice-A-Roni. And I'm talking all for one meal. My mother said it's always good to have a variety, plus my father was a cook in the army, so I only know how to cook for fifty or more. We ate until we were sick to our stomachs, and then took a midnight wade in the pool to work off the meal.

We were really enjoying our lives there, becoming L.A.'d out, but if you stay long enough in that town, eventually you are guilted into joining the gym. Excuse me, *spa*. I told Peter it was time we bit the bullet and joined up. In those days the gym was fast replacing the disco, and so, of course, I had to buy the appropriate outfits, ankle weights, and a good Walkman, not to mention the designer sneakers du jour. Well, ya don't want to ruin your arch, do ya?

The place was like Disneyland. All these neon lights and disco music. If only you didn't have to work out and get all sweaty, it would be really nice. Anyway, I marched myself right past the Lifecycles and into the juice bar. Wha? I was feeling a little peaked. Meanwhile, I was so impressed by the fat-free food that I think I put on a pound. I looked

Peter's mother getting a hug from Dennis Quaid.

My dad as a cook in the army! I can only make dinner for fifty.

down at the new waterproof sports watch I'd purchased just in case you're doing laps and have to know what time it is, and noticed that it was time to get my personalized exercise program. Well, two minutes into it, I got such a gas bubble lodged under my ribs. "Damn carrot juice!" I just couldn't concentrate, so I rescheduled with my trainer and went home to recuperate. That was the first and last time I ever went to the gym. So much for the lifetime membership.

It was time to start shooting *American Hot Wax*, the reason I was in L.A. The studio delivered a brand-new white Mustang convertible. On our first outing, Peter drove over a parking divider at the mall and completely wrecked the car. That was it. They're gonna fire me. What are we gonna do? Who do we call? But the next day the studio delivered a brand-new red one, no questions asked. I think I could get used to this.

The movie was going very well. Every time I spoke, people laughed. I wonder why? I hung out with Laraine Newman and

"American Hot Wax," my first lead in a film.

Me and Jay Leno,
"American Hot Wax."
Watch that hand, Jay.

Jay Leno. Peter and I loved the catered lunches. He used to get all dressed up in the white polyester *Saturday Night Fever* suit his mother had bought him for ten dollars at Odd Job Trading in Manhattan. We would sit in my trailer devouring the catered lunches like two piglets. Our only concern was whether or not we could get seconds on the potatoes. During my first kissing scene with Jay, Peter got really jealous.

"Did ya have to be so convincing? It's just a movie. I saw tongue. Why did I have to see tongue?"

Right there and then we set things straight. "I'm an actress. You're gonna have to get used to this, Pete, it means nothing to me ..."

Meanwhile, it was the best stage kiss I ever got. That Jay Leno is one damn good kisser. Maybe it has something to do with the chin.

The movie ended with a huge wrap party. It's sad, because you become a family and then you rarely ever see any of these people again. Peter and I decided to take the money I'd earned on the movie and stay in L.A. and try to get more work. The two of us were always lucky in that as soon as our debts got too big and we were getting too far in the red, out of the blue we'd get a job. Peter would book a commercial that we'd pray would run national (that's when ya get some big residual bucks). I remember when I got *Hollywood Knights,* costarring with a then unknown Michelle Pfeiffer, and I tell you, she was absolutely gorgeous. She wore these short shorts. In my life, the girl had the thinnest thighs I've ever seen. My mother thought they were too thin. She would.

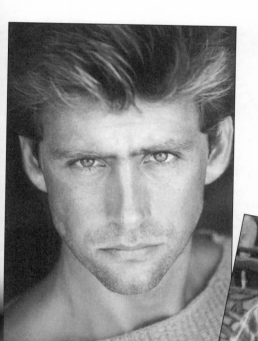

Peter tried working in his spare time as a model...for fifteen minutes.

Peter and Luke Perry on "Beverly Hills, 90210."

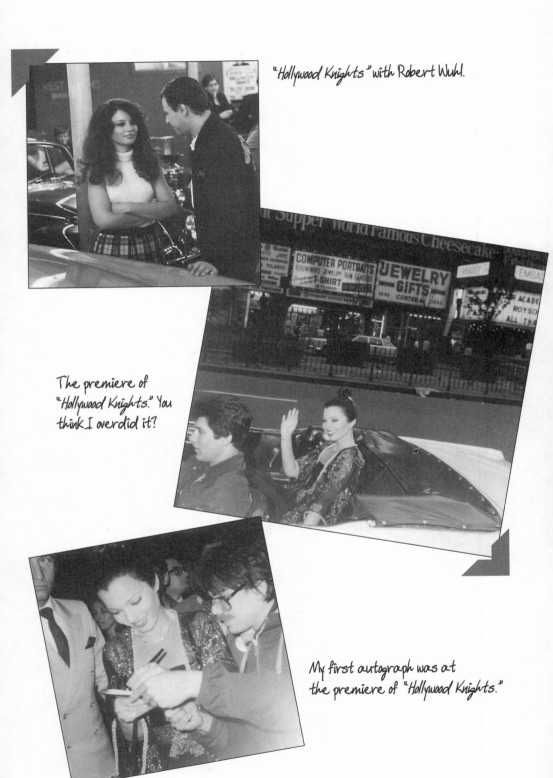

"Hollywood Knights" with Robert Wuhl.

The premiere of "Hollywood Knights." You think I overdid it?

My first autograph was at the premiere of "Hollywood Knights."

My parents insisted on coming out to make sure we weren't living in squalor. Ma told me to find a nice hotel for them for about fifteen dollars a night. Sure, Ma, we'll start with the Beverly Hills Hotel. Is she kidding? Eventually we found a place for forty dollars a night. The manager, a shlub wearing a white T-shirt covered in marinara sauce, showed us the room. Well, it was clean and tidy in an asylum sort of way, and it had a pool. We talked my parents into splurging on the room—"It's your vacation." But my mother was very disappointed when she found out it didn't come with a coffeemaker. "Call me silly, but with all the dough we're shelling out, it's the least they could do."

The day they arrived, I got the flu and passed it on to Peter, who passed it on to Ma, who gave it to my father. Plus, after a ten-year drought, L.A. experienced one of the worst rainstorms in recorded history. We all recovered the day it was time to take my parents back to the airport for their return flight. On the one day we were feeling a little better, my mother admired a mirror I'd bought at Bargain Circus. It had four yellow-and-orange men holding top hats painted on it. Real classy. My mother fell in love with it. "It's like your father and his brothers." Why, I don't know, but she wanted to have all the brothers' names painted on the mirror and take it back to New York. I told her to take it, with our blessing.

She found a place to paint all the names on it and couldn't believe how gorgeous it turned out, except they spelled Uncle Stanley's name wrong. It doesn't take much to please my mother. While packing it for the plane ride home, she insisted that the mirror was dirty and spritzed it with Windex. One by one all the names on the mirror started to smear. My mother, in a panic, grabbed a paper towel and tried to wipe up the Windex, but that only made it worse. You could hardly make out the names anymore, but Ma, through her tears, insisted it wasn't that bad and wanted it anyway.

While driving them to the airport we stopped at a Denny's

for some breakfast, ya know, because my mother can't eat before a flight (my parents like to take the "What's ya rush? You're retired!" morning flight for some reason). As we sit down, who is at the next table but Jack Palance. Oh, no, I thought, when my father, of course, immediately introduces himself, as does my mother, who has some egg hanging on her face.

"You're an actor, Jack, do you know my daughter?" Here we go. Jack was very sweet and answered all my dad's questions as my mother searched her pocketbook for her Instamatic.

"Oh, shit. I'm outta film," she mumbled. My parents apologized for bothering him as she sent my dad out for some film. And Jack went back to eating his waffles in peace. Everything was back to normal, until I noticed that my parents were smiling from ear to ear as they watched Jack eat. Like he was an attraction at Sea World. I'm surprised my mother didn't throw her lox in the air to see if he could catch it.

"Look at the time, we better go, we don't want to miss your flight," Peter hinted as we said our good-byes to Jack and pushed my parents back into the car. It was time to go.

Schmoozing with Milos Forman on the set of "Ragtime." You're sure I can't wear a little lipstick?

When we arrived at the airport, we unloaded the car and kissed my folks at the unloading zone. As Peter and I pulled away, my mother waved and cried, holding her paint-smeared mirror to her heart. I sat in the car, also crying. Peter suggested we go to the mall. Maybe that would cheer me up. Through my tears I agreed. I wasn't in a buying mood, but ya never know.

Chapter 4

The Wedding

Peter and I had been a couple for so many years that getting married seemed merely incidental. I mean, we did get engaged, but that was when we were back in Queens and everyone else was getting engaged, so it was kinda the thing to do. Peter had a

Peter and me at our engagement party. We were already like a forty-year-old couple.

Peter's parents, Pat and Ed. The best picture ever taken of them.

friend who had a father who had a business that worked with people who could get us a diamond wholesale. Now, we could have gone to Tiffany and bought a simple, tasteful stone, but we opted for what my mother refers to as "the bumba"—"over three carats." To the naked eye, it's gorgeous, but under a microscope, they're shoveling coal in there. But all my friends had bumbas on their fingers and Pretentious, I mean, Peter, wanted me to have a bumba, too. Me, I'm a joiner and went along with the program.

It was so weird, all these girls without a pot to piss in with these rocks on their hands. Meanwhile, I loved it, and we paid for it with the joint savings account Peter and I had started while we were still in high school. So I guess there was never a doubt that we were planning to be together. But once we moved to L.A., where all the hip were living together, there seemed no rush to get married. Of course, back in Queens I think it was getting on my parents' nerves.

"You bought a ring, we had a party, move your ass and get a blood test already. P.S., I wouldn't mind a grandchild who doesn't have four legs and eats Mighty Dog."

So one day, while thumbing through the latest issue of *Bride* magazine (I like the articles), something caught my eye. The most gorgeous, drop-dead wedding gown. Well, Peter

Me, Peter, and David Caruso at my wedding shower. One of our only friends when we moved to L.A. It was a very small shower.

thought the dress was unbelievable, too, and suggested I go to the bridal shop to try it on. I said, "Honey, a bridal shop isn't like going to Macy's and pulling a dress off the rack, it's a whole spiel, and one really shouldn't bother until one is getting married . . ."

"So, if you like the dress, we'll get married," he said. Wasn't that romantic? My entire future with this man rests on whether or not this wedding gown looks okay? When I called my mother and told her, she wept and told me through her tears that she "don't care if the dress looks like a sack of potatoes on. Tell him you love it." It so happens I did love it, even though it was a size ten, but with a little alteration . . .

My folks and Peter's parents were wonderful about planning the wedding and said they would help us make the arrangements and do whatever we wanted. The first discussion was the color scheme. "Well, since nobody likes to buy those gross wedding party dresses that they never wear again, why don't we do elegant black tie and evening gowns. This way the women can buy the black gown of their choice and wear it again as well." My mother's jaw dropped.

"BLACK!?" she shrieked. "You wanna put everyone in

black?? Did ya hear this, Morty?" What, no good, I thought. "Black is a funeral," my mother pontificated. "I won't come, and neither will Yetty (my grandmother)!" So after much deliberating we settled on navy, which my mother said was a good color and not a bad omen. But that was just the beginning of the dress mishegas, as my mother managed to create mayhem with each garment bought.

Now Peter's mom, without any hoopla, went out to Long Island and purchased a lovely navy dress. She looked the picture of elegance, although the general consensus from the women on my side of the family was that "at that age, sleeveless is not the way to go." In contrast, my mom had a friend who knew a friend who owned a wholesale house on Seventh Avenue in Manhattan, and ordered a dress that was multilayered chiffon, with a matching coat with beaded cuffs reminiscent of a Jewish Juliet. At the wholesale house, the gown was displayed as bone chiffon over white, but my mom, of course, ordered it in the politically correct navy over white, and proceeded to cry like a baby when the combination of colors turned the dress a garish baby blue. My dad said she could buy a new one, but my martyr, I mean, my mother, couldn't bear to waste the money. Besides, if they revised *Camelot,* she was all set to play Lady Guineverestein.

Now my sister, who would stand as my maid of honor, could not find a dress to save her life, which became an ongoing

Me and my sister, Nadine, wearing the dress my mother wanted to kill me over.

Michelle in the same gown Yetta wore to the wedding. Don't ask.

concern of my mother's until I finally suggested looking for something for Nadine in California. That was my first mistake, and the dress Nadine ultimately wore became the bane of my existence. From Polaroids of me modeling an absolutely lovely silk chiffon off-the-shoulder, fifteenth-century-looking romantic evening gown, the dress was bought and shipped. Now, all things being what they were, everyone seemed to be back on track until my friend Michelle, who would be my only bridesmaid, came to California for a visit.

Michelle also needed a gown, so we spent the better part of her vacation shopping for one. Eventually she ended up with a navy chiffon gown covered with an original hand painting of butterflies in flight, finished off with a large script "Michelle" painted on the chiffon right above knee level. Well, wouldn't ya know, just as soon as Michelle went home and Mom caught her first glimpse of this garish Tijuana special, she hit that phone and called California. If only she could have reached out and touched, I would surely be dead today!

"How could you let Michelle buy the same gown as Yetty?" How could there possibly be a second one? I thought, but my mother was serious.

"Ya know, she's borrowing her neighbor Blanche's dress that she wore to her sister's daughter's daughter's bat mitzvah!" she shrieked. "Okay, it has Blanche instead of Yetty painted on the chiffon, but nobody'll notice. The only difference is, it doesn't have the rhinestones!" And this is a bad thing? I thought. "Now Yetty and Michelle are gonna look like the Bobbsey twins walkin' down the aisle!"

Yetta's dress. The bane of
my existence.

"Relax, Ma, Yetty doesn't walk down the aisle," I reasoned.

"Oh, yeah," she mumbled under her breath, but was not beaten yet and forged ahead. "By the way, I hate Nadine's dress."

"Hate it? I thought ya loved it!" I was really confused now.

"It looked better in the picture, in person it looks like a nightgown, and my dress stinks, too. Who the hell picked navy?" Oy, I thought, we shoulda gone with black . . .

Next came the menu selection. We wanted the soup to be vichyssoise. "COLD POTATO SOUP? Feh!" was the feedback from Flushing, and matzo ball soup became the potage du jour. The same with the song for our first dance. It had been suggested that we pick a song, any song we liked that conveyed a special meaning. The *Lovers and Other Strangers* theme song sung by Karen Carpenter was our choice.

My mother began reciting the lyrics. "Love, look at the two of us, strangers in many ways . . ."

Then there was a long silence, which I finally broke with a simple "Yeah, so?"

"Well, what kind of a first dance song is that? Strangers in many ways? You're not strangers in many ways. Ya living together. Play 'More Than the Greatest Love the World Has Known'—that's a song!"

Getting ready for the Big Day.

Well, there was no way we were making that our song, and finally settled on "How Deep Is Your Love?" the Bee Gees song from *Saturday Night Fever*.

Well, finally it was a week before the wedding, and wouln't you know it, my mother got stung by a bee. There she was, minding her own business, walking home from the bus after work and feeling svelte after months of dieting in preparation for this auspicious occasion (the wedding), when out of nowhere a bee flew into her cleavage. Now, the poor bee took on more than he could chew and was probably suffocating within the depths of my mother's enormous breasts, while my mother, who hates bugs, began ripping open her blouse, tearing at her brassiere, and jumping, hopping, stomping, and screaming a sort of ritualistic dance that in other cultures might have brought on rain. Right there in the middle of Kissena Boulevard. Well, of course the bee stung her, and of course my mother was allergic. Her tits blew up to twice their normal size, resembling twin Goodyear blimps, and the news spread like wildfire throughout the family.

Needless to say, every yenta this side of Flushing called with a horror story of one person or another who had the unfortunate experience of getting stung by a bee and shortly thereafter dropping dead. My mom schlepped her watermelon breasts to the doctor at once.

"Bastard bee!" she exclaimed. "My mazel this should happen just the week before my wedding..." At this point my mother was openly and without hesitation referring to the affair as "her" wedding, and in almost every way it was. The doctor put her on antibiotics and topical ointments that helped clear up her reaction, and assured her that she would not die before Saturday night, but to this day, almost seventeen years later, when something lousy happens, we say "Bastard bee" and it somehow lightens the moment.

Well, Saturday night, November fourth, finally arrived, but not without further ado. The weather was freezing that day, and I arrived in my wedding dress with my winter coat (an Eddie Bauer parka) on top. My mother had had her hair done the day before and actually sat up all night in the living room chair

My wedding day. No black gowns. Ma's real happy.

in fear of deflation. But she was so hyped, nothing would ruin this night.

"Sorry, the lot's full," said the parking attendant as we pulled up to the valet, and like something out of a Fellini movie, my mother's whole face contorted into that of a mental patient with maniacal tendencies, and she began to scream, "FULL? How can the lot be full? I'm the first one here, where's my whole party gonna park?"

"We suggest your guests find a spot at either the gas station [he points diagonally across the street] or the car wash, which is right next door," he said, smiling as though this was some sort of consolation. Then, as if intending to be particularly

Peter kept telling the photographer to soften the lens. I was twenty-one at the time. Nu?

cruel and sadistic, he added, "Oh, by the way, you're not the first ones here, one of your guests already arrived, and they took the last spot on the lot."

As my father dropped Mom, me, and Peter off before finding a place to park at the car wash (my mother pushed him to hurry, before that lot got filled, too, and we'd have to park at the less desirable gas station across Queens Boulevard), I took in the absurdity of this enormous factory of affairs unfolding before my eyes as my warm breath turned to smoke in the bitter cold. Bar mitzvahs, anniversaries, weddings, and more weddings all seemed to be celebrated on November fourth. Some groups were Irish, some Italian, some Jewish, and with each party came more garish, glitzy, neon-colored ball gowns than the one before. Well, before long we realized it was Yetta's friend Jeany who was the first to arrive, which threw my mom into a bit of a tailspin.

"What the hell is Jeany doin' here? *I* haven't even arrived, and it's *my* party!" Peter tried to calm her down with a baby lamb chop from the hors d'oeuvres and cocktail room, which seemed to appease her, as she ripped the eye of meat off the little bone with her teeth while delicately holding the little paper booty with a raised pinkie.

Meanwhile, my uncle Dave, who was given the assignment of purchasing the cigars for the men after dinner, loaded up his car with several humidors and en route to the wedding decided to make a pit stop at a local corner newsstand and pick up a pack of cigarettes for himself, but made the unfortu-nate mistake of leaving the keys in the car and the car running. Not thirty seconds later the car and all the cigars were gone. My dad had to go pick him up as he stood stranded some ten blocks away, and, conse-quently, Dad had lost his precious car-wash spot by the time he returned with Uncle Dave; he didn't have much luck at the gas station either. So the two of them, after a long and arduous search, finally found a spot back at the newsstand, where they hailed a cab to the wedding.

The gown that got me hitched.

As the ceremony was about to begin, our rabbi popped a nitroglycerin pill under his tongue as we all held our breath. I mean, if the poor guy were to drop dead of a heart attack dur-ing our wedding ceremony it would put such a damper on the evening, and ya know they don't give refunds just because your rabbi bites the big one! While the electric piano played "Sunrise, Sunset," Mark, our best man, and my sister, wearing

My mother-in-law, Pat, in her understated dress (she ultimately opted for a chiffon shawl), and my mother in her Jewish Juliet.

her navy chiffon nightgown, began the procession, followed by Peter walking arm in arm with his parents half of the way, symbolizing the parents walking their child through the first part of life. He took his position under the chuppah, the tent one marries under in the Jewish faith, as did his dad, who neglected to put on his yarmulke, which became the big topic of discussion among some of the guests, and his mom, demure in her understated navy gown. She was followed by Michelle, looking more like Yetta than I would have thought possible, and as the pièce de résistance, a curtain opened to reveal me, my mom, and my dad, silhouetted behind another sheer curtain dramatically backlit by a golden halo. Then the second curtain opened, and we began our ascent toward the chuppah. It was like I was debuting at the Riviera Hotel in Vegas. "When did she get to be a beauty? When did he grow to be so tall?" crooned the musician. There wasn't a dry eye in the house. My dad's lips had already begun to chap from standing and waiting for that cab. I, in the middle, felt pretty and stupid all at the same time, and my mom, who seemed more like a bride than the bride, floated down the aisle, a vision in Corning Ware blue.

Well, aside from some uncontrollable laughter on my part during the ceremony, things went pretty smoothly, the rabbi lived, and ten minutes later we were husband and wife. At the

Peter's family.

reception, Peter and I worked the room, moving from table to table, posing with guests for the photographer, and boy, were my shoes killing me. I remember that I had just sat down to enjoy my chateaubriand, kicked my shoes off my swollen feet, at this point resembling the feet of a Cabbage Patch doll, when I noticed that my sister had accidentally leaned a little too close to the candelabra centerpiece and had set her hair on fire. Well, without skipping a beat, I grabbed the celery dish and dumped it on her head. The ice from the dish put out the flames, and my sister spent the next hour picking radish out of her wiglet.

By the end of the night, we had all managed to gorge ourselves on the "Viennese table," a synonym for "Put every lousy dessert they make on a buffet and give it a European name." Afterward I was so tired, and my feet throbbed, so when my dad pulled the car around, I

My family.

The day after the wedding. I wasn't kidding. We stayed in my old room on the high-riser.

sat my ass in the back-seat, kicked off my shoes, and waited while all the hoopla died down outside. Peter and my dad were loading the trunk with gifts received, my mom kissed people, and when it was all over no one knew where I'd gone until they spotted a round white head through the rear window of the car. Mom, Dad, and Peter piled in the car and we all drove home. Peter and I spent our wedding night on the high-riser in my old bedroom. We wouldn't have had it any other way.

David Caruso and friend found our wedding picture in the window of the photographer's in Queens, New York.

Chapter 5

Elaine

A month or two after moving to Los Angeles, Peter connected with a theatrical manager named Elaine Rich. She was from New York, had a great sense of humor, a wonderful sense of style, and a voice that rivaled mine (no

On our terrace, dressed for our first big party at Elaine's.

wonder he loved her). Shortly thereafter, Elaine invited us to our first big Hollywood party. Dressed to the nines, we entered her Spanish-style duplex apartment. Of course, everyone was in chic, basic black while we looked like Sonny and Cher.

Avant-garde art filled the walls, Calder mobiles hung from the ceilings, booze and food were free-flowing, and everyone from Tom Selleck (who was on my favorite soap opera at the time) to Rene Russo (who was a famous model in those days) was sprawled on Elaine's overstuffed furnishings (oh, if only I'd brought my Polaroid Swinger). The combination of a white-wine spritzer and a tilted bladder put me badly in need of a bathroom, but oddly enough, it was always occupied, and there seemed to be several voices coming from behind the locked door. Talk about a spastic colon, I thought, and in vain offered my Pepto-Bismol to the eight sniffling people who were exiting. What is it, allergy season? All right, so I was naive in those days.

I had just shoved a piece of honey-baked ham in my face when much to my and Peter's shock, one of the guests (a famous celebrity who shall remain nameless) got so blitzed on booze, and God knows what else, that she passed out right in the middle of the living room floor. But I tell you, my hand to God, no one even noticed. They didn't even bother to pick her up. They all continued in their own worlds, quite unfazed. Mind you, this was Hollywood in the eighties, when people threw wild parties. But we had never seen anything like this where we came from, because where we came from the sight of a passed-out party guest would have ignited mass hysteria of

Elaine and Allan's wild days.

four-alarm proportions, followed by sixteen Jews all screaming at the 911 operator.

Meanwhile, Elaine sashays out from the kitchen and stops at the body as if it were a parking bumper and announces, "Come and get it, dinner is served!" And without skipping a beat, she yells to her husband, "Allan, would you pick her up? She's blockin' the buffet."

So as Allan schlepped the actress over to the side and propped her on the couch, Peter and I made a beeline for the food. This was some spread, I thought, as we loaded up our plates like when we were at the Sizzler salad bar. Peter introduced me to Elaine as Fran Drescher, but Elaine qualified me as being Sheryl Berkowitz of *American Hot Wax*, to which I modestly said, "Guilty!"

"Honey, the whole town's talkin' about you," she enthused, at which point I nearly choked on a chicken wing but tried to remain cool.

"That's nice," I uttered before gulping a Perrier to wash down the wing. It was love at first sight; needless to say, by week's end she had signed me on as a client, and we've all been together ever since.

Dennis Quaid and me imitating Allan and Elaine.

Now, I credit my parents for building me the kind of loving, supportive foundation on which I have been able to experience and digest, in a healthy and self-confident way, the rest of my life, but by nineteen or twenty years of age, I needed another kind of influence to help broaden Peter and me, expose us to the levels of culture and worldliness we hungered for. This was where Elaine and her husband, Allan, played a most pivotal role. They had both spent a lot of time in therapy, the art world, and Europe, and they shared with us their insights, helping to expand our way of thinking about things. Not to mention pointing us toward the best bagels and lox in town.

Allan, an intelligent man of great diversity, accomplished not only as an actor but also as an art dealer, a collector, and a stockbroker, liked to debate issues with us, always challenging our thought processes. But Elaine is in a class of her own. Peter and I attribute all our success to this most amazing woman. She always believed in us, many times footing the bill for expenses we incurred as actors (e.g., photos) but could not afford. It was she who encouraged Peter to move into writing and producing, and she who was always there in our hours of need.

Elaine, like my mother, is naturally funny without really trying. I'll never forget after Sarah Vaughan had just passed away from lung cancer and Elaine took a long draw off her Carlton cigarette, saying, in deep denial, "All that singing can't be good!" There was always something to laugh about when Peter, Elaine, and I got together. Even at my most humiliating auditions we'd find humor.

I remember once I was auditioning for a singing waitress in a pilot, and Elaine came over to our house to see what progress I'd made in preparing for the audition (basically, because singing is not exactly my forte). Well, Peter played the piano and I sang for Elaine as best I could, when Elaine cut me off in the middle.

"Ya know what, honey, go put on your makeup and what ya plan to wear, let me see the whole look." But an hour later, fully made-up and dressed, my voice didn't sound any better. Then a brainstorm.

"Ya know what, honey, when ya get to the lyric 'it all depends on you,' say the producer's name, Al Burton, and

Elaine and Peter.

point your finger at him, that oughta grab him."

Okay, that could be cute, I thought, so I tried it. "It all depends on *YOU* [point], Al Burton . . ." Both Peter and Elaine sat there, dumbfounded. "What, no good?" I questioned. Peter and Elaine remained speechless. "Should I skip the point part, is it an overkill?" I asked innocently, when suddenly Elaine broke the silence.

"Ya know what, honey, what we need is some schwarma," and the three of us, while stuffing ourselves on Middle Eastern food, decided that since I'd never "laid a stink bomb" (Elaine's term for a lousy audition), why start now? And the audition was canceled.

In a similar vein, I auditioned for the *Fame* series and had to sing for them as well, but in this instance I was actually offered the role in the pilot, in which I was to sing a solo number. Wow! I actually beat out all my friends who were professional singers. Elaine whispered to Peter, "What are they, deaf?" and off to New York we went to shoot the pilot. I diligently rehearsed my song with Michael Gore, anticipating the day I was to shoot my big singing scene.

The day came, and I belted my best rendition of "You Are My Lucky Star" when suddenly the director, quite irate, questioned me with "WHAT ARE YOU DOING?"

Couldn't he tell I was singing? My heart sank as I responded, "Well, I've been practicing as hard as I could, but I guess I didn't sound very good, huh?"

Our version of
"The Blue Lagoon,"
Jewish style.

To which he snapped, "You sound *too* good, I want you to sing off-key like you did at the audition!" When *Fame* got picked up, my option didn't.

In spite of such mishaps, Elaine, Peter, and I kept trying to finagle our way into the big time. Elaine had a friend who knew the editor of *New York* magazine, and without any plan in mind, cocktails were arranged. Now, I'm sure this guy was just doing his friend a favor and never expected anything to come of it, but the more Peter and I chatted about high school and show business, the more intrigued he became. And a very clever human interest story was published, all about how Peter and I were two kids from Queens on the fast track toward becoming, as the article was titled, "The Lucy & Desi of the 80's" (all right, so they were off by a decade).

Now, a very prominent producer (who shall also remain nameless) read the article and expressed an interest in meeting us. "We'll feed him, that's what we'll do!" I shouted while taking an inventory of lasagne ingredients in my pantry. "We'll eat, we'll schmooze, we'll sell him our ideas!"

So me, Peter, Elaine, and what's-his-name all sat around the kitchen table as the smell of my lasagne perfumed the air. The guy seemed to enjoy talking about himself (what a surprise), and since his reputation for being quite flamboyant and outrageous had preceded him, we three were not short on questions. Suddenly the guy announced that his feet were cold.

"I beg your pardon, did you just say your feet are cold?" I asked with incredulity. Elaine, who had just shoved a cracker with a mound of chopped liver in her mouth, widened her eyes as the producer pulled out from under the table an enormous leg and presented this fat, naked foot stuffed into an Italian loafer. Peter kindly suggested that he would get a pair of his own sweat socks for the producer to wear, which he did, and for the moment the crisis was aborted. We waited on this shlub hand and foot, trying to move on to the order of business, when just as I reached in the oven to remove the most delicious, bubbling-hot lasagne (my standard enough-to-feed-fifty-people size), this cretin passed out in his pâté.

"Oh, my God, is he dead?" I questioned, an oven mitt on each hand as I held a sixty-pound casserole.

Just then he seemed to be coming around, and Elaine mumbled, "Boy, this is one for the memoirs," and Peter asked him if he needed a doctor.

"No, I just need to lie down for a minute." He assured us that this happened quite often, to which Elaine mumbled under her breath, "Cover the couch, he's full of liver!"

Peter walked him to the couch, where he crashed. Back in the kitchen, the three of us wondered what to do and decided there's only one thing to do . . . eat the lasagne! Hey, it was getting cold. A few hours later the man got up, got into his sports car, and sped off. We were never to see him or Peter's sweat socks again. Oh, well, back to the drawing board.

Chapter 6

Spinal Tap

My look for "Spinal Tap":
a little bit country,
a little bit Diana Ross.

It was during the shooting of *Doctor Detroit,* the Dan Aykroyd picture for Universal Studios, when I first heard of a small but noteworthy project titled *This Is Spinal Tap.* This was to be Rob Reiner's directing debut in features, and Norman Lear's company was going to produce it. Rob was getting some really talented people to play various different roles, and Elaine felt that this project was right up my alley. Peter thought it seemed perfect because I had a habit of getting into projects that were offbeat, experimental, and, most consistently, paid little or no money. Since *Spinal Tap* seemed to fit the bill, I was a shoo-in.

The basis of the movie was to create a really satirical look, with a documentary feel to it, at a rock band on the road. Rob would play the documentary filmmaker following the English band Spinal Tap making its comeback tour. I was meeting Rob for the part of Bobbi Flekman, the record promoter for the label that was sponsoring the tour. The only day Rob could meet me was the day after a night shoot on *Doctor Detroit.* I was so tired, but somehow my exhaustion paid off for me, because Rob really responded to my slow, monotone, I-could-give-a-shit-I'm-so-fuckin'-tired attitude.

He said, "You're not what I was expecting, or how I saw the character."

"I think I'm a little tired, I've been shooting nights all week," I said in my own defense.

"No, I like it,

Lydia Lei, Donna Dixon, me, and Lynn Whitfield. Four hos in "Doctor Detroit."

it's very interesting," he said, like the genius that he is, and booked me to play the part. I didn't know at the time that this little low-budget film with its first-time director (Archie Bunker's Meathead) would be a turning point in my career, but that's exactly what it became.

Behind the scenes in "Doctor Detroit" before four hours of makeup.

I had about two weeks left to go on *Doctor Detroit* and then would begin straightaway on *Spinal Tap*. I'll tell ya, it's a lesson to be learned during one's career that work brings work, so be reticent about turning down anything. The money offered on *Spinal Tap* was so low, it's a good thing we were hard up (no matter how low, it was more than unemployment), or I might have passed. But I didn't, and what a break it was. That little low-budget picture—I don't think it cost even a million dollars—continues to this day, over a decade later, to be revered as one of the

On "Doctor Detroit" with way too much time on our hands.

greatest films about the music industry and is considered a cult classic.

There were no dressing rooms, no costumes, no money, and no script. Most people don't realize that *This Is Spinal Tap* was a completely improvised movie. Each actor was given a twenty-five-page outline pointing out any key information that needed to be covered in each scene; after that, what was said and how we got to the plot point was anyone's guess. All told, I think I worked three or four days. I wore my own clothes and did my own hair and makeup. But I, unfortunately, developed a bad cold and was quite miserable throughout the shoot.

The first day we shot there was a general discussion on what we could and couldn't say. They didn't want lawsuits, so anything slanderous was a no-no. I remember sitting around with Michael McKean, Chris Guest, and Harry Shearer (Michael and Chris I worked with again years later in a movie Chris directed called *The Big Picture*, starring Kevin Bacon), and I questioned whether I could mention to the band to check the IDs of groupies because I didn't wanna Roman Polanski on my hands.

"Oh, yeah, that you can say," they all agreed with enthusiasm; that was just the type of stuff they were looking for. Man, when they put on the wigs, the costumes, and those English accents, they no longer were themselves but were an authentic English rock band.

It was amazingly impressive even for those on the inside who watched it happen. And when I shot the scene with the band's manager (played by Tony Hendra) where I tell him that the image of a naked, greased woman in a dog collar on all fours being forced to smell the glove on the album cover is too sexist and that certain mainstream stores are boycotting it, the actor doing the improv with me tried to explain to me that that's what sells albums, to which I responded, "What about *The White Album* by the Beatles, there was nothing on that goddamned cover!"

Well, when we finished the scene, Rob ran up to me with such adulation. He was so thrilled that I'd brought up *The White Album*. It was perfect, he said, and asked if I knew.

"Knew what?" I said, bewildered, blowing my nose from the cold. Then he proceeded to explain that the album cover controversy extends throughout the story, and by the end of the film the next Spinal Tap album is released with a solid-black cover. Well, I didn't know, but I was thrilled that I could make him so happy. To this day there is a familial bond among the *Spinal Tap* alumni. Besides the band and Rob, Billy Crystal, Dana Carvey, Paul Shaffer, and Bruno Kirby are just a few of the more illustrious players with whom I always exchange a heartfelt hello and a hug.

All told, Rob ended up with nine and a half hours of film footage that would be cut down to an hour and a half. Honestly, I was lucky I had the two great scenes I had left in the film; others never made the final cut and ended up on the cutting-room floor.

It's funny, but all indications were that *Doctor Detroit*, the big-star, big-budget, major studio–release picture would be the big break

The billboard of "Doctor Detroit." It was so exciting when we saw it at Universal Studios that we took out the camera. Always carry it. Ya never know.

"Doctor Detroit," where Dan and Donna met. I played Cupid.

for me, but the best thing that came out of that movie was our friendship with Donna Dixon and Dan. Did I mention that I was the one who kinda got those two together? Yup. Most of the time, shooting with Dan was spent talking about Donna, with whom Peter and I had become instant friends. Dan fell for her like a ton of bricks and would express his desire to cradle

her beautiful face in his hands, which, of course, I reported back to her, and around and around we went throughout the filming, until one evening after a wonderful dinner at our house, on my front porch, Dan Aykroyd proposed to Donna Dixon and she accepted.

But it was the suc-

Me and Dan.

cess of *Spinal Tap,* and its critical acclaim, that I coasted on as an actress for years. Everyone who was anyone in the film, TV, and music industries knew who I was because of my character, Bobbi Flekman. More often than not the greatest compliment I received was when people admitted that they thought I was a real person and not an actress playing a part. And the most prestigious award I ever received (besides, of course, being voted left-hander of the year) was when *Esquire* magazine awarded me their five-minute Oscar given to those actors deserving of an Oscar but unable to qualify due to the size of their parts.

My first Bob Mackie. He was such a doll, he lent it to me.

Peter and Donna.

Chapter 7

The Rain in Spain

Among the questions I get asked the most are, Is this my real voice? and, Did I ever try to lose my accent? Please. Who would make this voice up? Well, once when times were slow and jobs were scarce, Elaine called me up and said she wanted to do lunch. I had no sooner ordered my pasta primavera when the first words outta her mouth were, "Honey, ya gotta do something about the voice." Not even "Ya want some bread?" She always hits you with the bad news first, clears the air, then she can enjoy lunch. "Like a good surgeon, one clean amputation and it's over," Elaine says. "Whereas a bad one keeps cutting a little piece at a time and makes a big mess of things."

"Honey," she said, "you're limiting yourself with your voice."

"Whaddaya mean? I can do Spanish, I can do Italian, French."

"Yeah, but it's the American I'm having trouble selling."

Well, I think I've just been insulted. I'm ordering an expensive dessert. So there. Now, Peter always thought my voice was what made me unique. I preferred Peter's take on the situation. But Elaine insisted that I listen to her and seek help from a voice specialist to eliminate my, shall we say, nasal nuance.

I'll tell ya, I was so taken aback I could hardly finish my meal. I mean, I managed, but it wasn't easy. "Honey, you'll still be able to use your accent when you need it. But you'll also be able to play all those other normal-sounding people."

"Oh, come on, it doesn't sound that weird!" A sudden silence fell upon the table. "Oh, all right, I'll go." I made an appointment that week.

I felt like Eliza Doolittle. I was to be the doctor's greatest challenge since Dolph Lundgren. I saw the doctor once or twice a week. I was doing pretty well, but talking a little slow, sounding like Meryl Streep on a quaalude. In fact, Dr. Glass called it my low, slow, flow voice. Eventually, when I got accustomed to speaking properly I'd speed it up and get to play all those great roles that I never got a chance to go up on. But for now I had to settle for sounding like Darth Vader. When I went home I'd diligently do my exercises, but ten minutes later I was talking through my nose again. What did they want from me? It wasn't natural. Plus, I lost my whole personality.

Well, lo and behold, Elaine did get me an audition for a normal-sounding person. In fact, I had worked for these producers before. Wait till they get a load of the new me. Two seconds into auditioning for the part, the producers had a shit fit.

"What did you do to your voice?"

"Huh?"

"We want the real you."

Oy. Oh, all right. I did it again, but I was lost. I think I forgot how to do it. It was somewhere between Julie Andrews and

I had an audition for Jean Harlow.
Whaddaya think?

Still toying with my Jean Harlow look...

Debra Nadoodleman designed
this for me in "Three Amigos."
Unfortunately, they cut
forty-five minutes of the film,
and I was one of those minutes.

Rosie Perez. I left, but not defeated. Maybe I just hadn't worked out all the kinks yet.

The phone rang again, this time for the lead in *The Winds of War*, a miniseries. They loved my look, and I thought the audition went pretty well, but after we hadn't heard anything for about a month, and they were already filming in Europe, I was beginning to get the idea that they'd gone with someone else. Elaine called the casting director for some feedback. She said, "Her voice was great, but it took her so long to get a sentence finished. The miniseries is only eight hours, Elaine!"

Well, that was the straw that broke the adenoid's back. It's either nasal or nothing!

My audition for "Winds of War"—before they heard me speak.

Can you make it any bigger?

Chapter 8

Surgery

It's funny how in life everything can be going along hunky-dory, and then one day, without warning, you get kicked in the ass. It was during a routine exam at my gynecologist's that he discovered a lump in my breast. Now, I have a family history on my mother's side of benign tumors, but I had never before discovered one in myself.

Very matter-of-factly, the man said, "Do you know you have a lump in your right breast?"

"No, no, I didn't."

I had no idea, but within minutes he had sent me to this oncologist who worked on another floor in the same medical building. He tried to aspirate (drawing a fluid cyst out with a needle), but the damned thing was bone-dry and as hard as a rock.

"I'd like to schedule you for surgery as soon as possible," he said. "Probably nothing to be alarmed about, I'm sure it's benign considering your age and history, but still, it's best to get it out of there and get it biopsied."

Was this really happening? I thought. My mind raced. Jesus Christ, I just went in for a pap test and now I'm being scheduled for surgery. I'd never had surgery before. Not even had my tonsils removed, and now this. When, was the obvious next question as he checked over his calendar.

"We've got Memorial Day weekend coming up, and no openings before that, so why don't we just set you up for outpatient surgery a week from Wednesday."

I have to wait till after the holiday? Happy Memorial Day! It seemed like an eternity. Nothing but time to ponder the possible consequences of this predicament. True, the odds were in my favor, but I've heard women on TV, young women with mastectomies, who've said they were told the same thing.

That night we went home to our apartment and I dove into the pool and swam. Back and forth, back and forth, trying not to fall apart and think the worst. Not to get consumed with negative energy or thoughts. So I swam powerfully, back and forth, back and forth, and tried not to cry. That week to follow was a long one, but thank goodness I had that Memorial Day weekend barbecue to look forward to. We had invited one of our favorite couples over to spend the day with us and I was looking forward to making all my favorite recipes. Unfortunately, they canceled out for a weekend in Acapulco, and I was devastated. The only thing that was getting me through this was taken away, and we ended up at Elaine's house instead.

Curiously enough, there were little, insignificant things that seemed to keep happening that reinforced in my mind that I was rapidly disappearing. People would address Peter but fail to notice me standing there. Calls would come in but never for me. I had a heightened awareness of how simply I could just be lifted out of the picture, just removed from the equation as easily and neatly as that. At Elaine's I expressed how hurt I was by my friend's insensitivity to my situation, and remembered how I agonized for her well-being when she'd had a tumor removed just a few months before. It was Elaine who set me straight on a few matters about friends and expectations. That Memorial Day weekend at Elaine's I learned one of the more valuable lessons in my life: Know before whom thou stands. Understand your friends for who they are, not who you wish them to be. Accept them for their flaws as well as their attributes. Turn to them for their strengths, what good stuff they can bring to your life, and forget about the rest. To ask for more only sets you up for failure.

Now, Elaine is a wise old owl, and we understood what she was saying. For example, it was true that these particular friends had a habit of last-minute cancellations, but in so many ways they were such wonderful, generous, fun-loving people. So how to deal with the frustration of never really knowing if you've got plans or not? Simply never expect them to keep their commitment. Coordinate plans that will be able to continue with or without them. And if I drop dead, boy, will they feel guilty. From that point on we would tell them, "This is what we're doing, if you'd like to join us, you're more than welcome." Sometimes they'd come, sometimes they wouldn't, but it never mattered again. Because that weekend unfolded the way it did, Peter and I became far more tolerant and independent friends to our friends. Consequently, we remain good friends with so many wonderful people, some for almost twenty years.

When the day came that I was scheduled for outpatient surgery, it all seemed so unreal. Peter and I had to separate as they wheeled me off to the OR. Everything seems strange. The faces you don't recognize who talk you through the procedure, the halls along the way, the smells of medicine and illness. Once in the operating room, an area of a hospital I'd never been in before, a small dividing curtain was placed between my neck and breast. I guess they think you'll freak out if you see them slicing into your flesh. To this day I find it hard to believe, but they actually perform the surgery with only the aid of Novocain. And, honey, I was expecting to be knocked out like never before. Instead, several shots were administered into my breast until it was a mass of numb tissue. When the doctor asked if I could feel anything, at first I panicked and thought I could.

"Don't cut yet, don't cut yet," I shouted, but it was only the pressure I felt and not an actual feeling of pain.

I yakked from nerves through the whole thing, cracking everyone up with my motormouth. It turned out that there were two tumors found, which were placed in a stainless-steel bowl and carted off by the nurse to be diagnosed.

"We'll have them biopsied, but they look clean to me," said the surgeon.

Ya know, you are asked to sign a permission form in the event that it looks bad and the doctor deems it necessary to do a radical. I opted to sign the release, figuring that whatever the situation, I would not want to be sewed up only to have long discussions when I knew I'd want it removed, and then have to endure going under the knife again!

They wheeled me into recovery, where I lay on the gurney I was operated on right next to a young woman who had just gotten out of her own surgery. The only thing I remember about her was that she was craving pizza and couldn't wait to go home and order some. P.S., the power of suggestion is a mighty powerful thing, and sure enough, I, too, couldn't wait to get home and order a pizza.

When they wheeled me into the waiting room, I began to laugh to myself as I recalled the time Peter had had some out-patient surgery. He had been so nervous that the nurse had given him an extra-heavy dose of Valium to calm him down before the operation. Now, it turned out that a very big call-back for a movie was scheduled for later that day, so I arranged for Judi, one of our oldest and dearest friends, to stay with Peter at home for an hour while I ran over to my audition. She couldn't get there until after two, but that was okay, since the meeting wasn't until two-thirty. So, if at one they said he'd be ready to go home, that should give me plenty of time to get back to the house, set Peter up in bed, wait for Judi, and then rush over to the callback. When I arrived the nurse led me to a private recovery room where Peter was resting.

"He's still a little drugged from all the Valium," explained the nurse.

"What do ya mean? Can't ya get him up?" I asked.

"Well, not really," she said. "He could probably rest a couple more hours before the drug wears off."

"But I don't have a couple of hours. I have this big callback. Now, come on, help me get him up, honey!"

I began nervously trying to get his socks and shoes on over his size-eleven boats and shouted to the nurse, "Sit him up! Sit him up! We gotta get outta here."

With all my strength I hoisted Peter up off the recovery cot and dumped him in the wheelchair that would roll him to the curb. The poor guy was like a big piece of Jell-O, and I wasn't exactly Florence Nightingale, but I had a mission, and believe me, if Peter could speak, I'm sure he'd be the first to say the surgery's over, and we could use the movie to pay next year's rent!

With one hand I held on to his wavering body as I opened the car door with the other and plopped him in the front seat, buckling him in so he literally wouldn't fold over. The whole way home he whined and moaned inaudibly, but I discovered that he seemed to enjoy the chocolate I continued to shove in his mouth from outta the bottom of my purse. When we finally got home, I steered all six feet, two hundred pounds of him up the front path as chocolate dribbled from his mouth. It was lovely. As we entered the house, he wanted to sit down.

"Not now, honey. If you go down, there's no turning back.

Well, we did it, babe, and now you're home, back in your own bed, safe and sound . . ." I said lovingly as I tied him to the bed so he wouldn't fall out.

But now it was my turn to be the patient. As I entered the waiting room I saw Peter there, anxious to hear how I was.

"They say it looks like nothing to worry about."

He thanked God and helped me into the car. Now, the packing they cover you with was so thick it looked like a football player's chest pad, plus the weight alone of a woman's breast manages to put an automatic stress on the stitched flesh, so all in all, I was miserable. But not as miserable as I became when that Novocain began to wear off. Holy shit. This was a pain I had never felt before and hope never to feel again. The incision goes so deep, and somehow you can feel the depth of the slice of the knife. While waiting in the car for my pain pills in the pharmacy parking lot, I thought I was gonna die. The pain became rapidly more intense as I caught sight of Peter exiting from the store with my prescription.

Once I was home and fully loaded on Percodan, Peter propped me up in the den and ordered me a large cheese pizza. Well, I hadn't been home an hour when the phone started ringing off the hook. Guess everyone wanted to see how I was doin', well, guess again. By some amazing coincidence, a huge cover story had broken in the *Enquirer* tabloid revealing the up till now secret marriage of Danny Aykroyd and Donna Dixon. Not one person started the conversation with "Is she all right?" but rather, "Is it true?" What a joke, there I sat bandaged like an Egyptian mummy, two huge tumors removed, I'd probably gotten by within an inch of my life, and Danny and Donna, without even trying, had upstaged my surgery. Thank goodness I am such an accepting and understanding friend to my friends, I thought, as I gorged myself on a cheese and pepperoni pizza!

Chapter 9

Warren

It was springtime in L.A. Not too hot or rainy, but warm and breezy. We were house-sitting for Danny and Donna this one Saturday and had invited a few of my girlfriends over for the afternoon to lie around the pool when Elaine called to tell me about a last-minute audition being held at the Sunset Marquis Hotel in Westwood. "On a SATURDAY??" I whined.

"Honey, you're meeting Warren Beatty and Elaine May, now get your ass outta bed!" Elaine succinctly responded, and I did.

The movie was the now infamous *Ishtar,* but at the time, this film with the strange name starring Warren Beatty and Dustin Hoffman, directed by Elaine May, was creating quite a stir. Warren, who was also producing, was costarring with his real-life girlfriend (at the time), French actress Isabelle Adjani, as the female lead, so I and several other hopeful actresses would be reading for the roles of the women Hoffman and Beatty leave behind in New York before venturing to Ishtar! Nu? Always a bridesmaid, never a bride.

There was no script being released ahead of time. They implied that it was a security thing to protect the script from getting into the hands of rip-off artists, but, in retrospect, the script was probably in turmoil even back then, and there was probably *no* script. So the plan was that I get there a little early and study my part right before going in to read.

All I knew about the part was that it was Dustin Hoffman's girlfriend, who he refuses to marry and eventually dumps. Well, since I figured the girl he dumps must be a pathetic loser, and since I was neither and probably would never get cast in such a part, I decided to take the meeting with the sole intention of meeting Warren and Elaine, ya know, for future projects more suited for a pretty, Jewish girl with a good figure and a voice that could call the cows home. I decided to wear this orange, slinky dress with a sexy belt slung over my hips and a pair of strappy sandals that one of the girls had worn over to Donna's pool that day. Peter stayed at the Aykroyd house with our friends, and I hopped in the car and wound my way through the canyon tingling with exhilaration because I was going to meet Warren Beatty.

When I got there, I had to wait and work on my part in the hotel lobby. I must have checked myself in the mirror a thousand times, and then someone called my name and directed me up to the audition suite. My heart was pounding as I watched the elevator numbers light up, and then it stopped. The doors opened and I stepped out. When I located the room and knocked on the door, Elaine May answered it. She was a dark, thin woman, unkempt and eccentric in her appearance. Her hair was black and gray. She smoked a cigar and bits of it clung to her lips.

"Hi, I'm Elaine May. Come in, did they tell you we're putting you on tape?"

She was driving the meeting, trying to move things along. They were running about an hour late with their appointment schedule. As she led me into the room, I focused on him. Our eyes locked. He has this way of looking right into your soul, making you feel like he is totally focused on no one but you. And the way he looked. I kept thinking that this was not a young man, but in many ways better-looking than when he did *Splendor in the Grass* when he was so very young and gorgeous and luscious—and I'm getting off track here. I also really have a great deal of respect for him as a producer and director, both responsibilities beautifully exemplified by the movie *Reds*.

So this experience was having an impact on many levels, but, oh, that impish grin. Hello, honey! A young man's grin, more specifically the grin on the face of a boy, and clear blue eyes that twinkled. I thought it was nothing more than that winning grin and those eyes that managed to seduce all those women from whom he gained the reputation of being such a ladies' man.

"Hello Warren, are you gorgeous, I'm Fran Drescher, and I'm so happy to meet you," I found myself saying.

"Dustin couldn't be here, so I'll be reading his part with you," he said.

"Hey, I don't have a problem with that!" I was brimming with adulation.

Elaine interjected, "Do you have any questions, Fran?" still trying to move things along.

What I didn't realize then was that the cosmic connection I felt Warren and I were experiencing was probably experienced by every starlet who was auditioning that day. Hence the reason for their running an hour behind. Hence Elaine moving things along.

"Well, I was wondering what the movie was about and how my character fits into the plot?"

Her response really blew my mind, as she proceeded to tell me the whole story from my character's point of view: "It's about a girl who's been dating this one guy for a couple of years and he tells her he loves her but then acts distant and says he's not ready to make a commitment, which of course ends with him breaking up with her, which breaks her heart. The last thing she heard of him was that he was off to visit a place called Ishtar."

Then Elaine May looked at me, deadpan, and quite matter-of-factly stated, "It isn't necessary to know more than your character would know."

Wow, was I ever impressed. She was absolutely right, and what a refreshing approach to a character. The woman is a genius, I thought, as I was engulfed by the smoke of her cigar.

Now, the scene I was about to do with Warren was the moment when Hoffman breaks up with me in my story. Bummer, no kiss . . . I felt like we worked well together, and I was very honest as the character. He reached for me, I slapped his arm and pulled away. I grabbed my throat to keep from crying, not wanting to expose the pain in front of the man who was causing it. It was a dramatic scene that seemed to ignite with life as I acted with Warren.

When it was over he looked at me and said, "Who are you? You're really good. What have you done? Where did you study?"

Boy, if I thought he liked me before . . . Just as I was about to open my mouth, Elaine kinda answered him for me.

"She's terrific, Warren. That was really great"—this she threw to me. "We must move on."

Now, as if it were a test of wills between Elaine May and Warren, he turned to me and said, "I'll walk you to the elevator. We can talk on the way." Then, "Why don't you call for the next actress, Elaine."

Yeah, Elaine, call the next actress, I thought.

As we walked down the hallway, he was so complimentary about everything. "I think you're a tremendous talent."

"Warren, I can't believe you're telling me this, wait till I tell Peter. Oh, I wish I had a tape recorder, no one is gonna believe Warren Beatty told me I—"

"Who's Peter?" he interrupted.

"Oh, Peter's my husband. We've been together since we were fifteen years old."

Suddenly he reached into his pocket and pulled out a pen and paper, and as he started jotting something down, said, "I'd like to get to know you and Pete better," then, handing me the paper, "here's my private number. Give me a call." Above the number he wrote his initials, W.B. Then he added, "Sometimes I gather some friends together. Jack"—Jack Nicholson? I thought—"my attorney, a small group, and we screen a film and have dinner. Call me toward the end of the week, and if I'm doin' one, I'd love you and Pete to come." All I could say was "Okay!"

"By the way," he said.

"Yes," I said (my heart at this point was fibrillating with excitement and all my mouth could form was one-word answers).

"I think I know your husband. What's he do?"

"He's an actor and a writer, but you don't know him—"

But W.B. persisted. "Are you sure? Because I think I might have met him once."

Then he ran his hand through this dark, wavy hair that was long enough to hang over his shirt collar, when I reiterated (as I began to realize this man is incapable of being anything but adorable), "Warren, trust me, you don't know Peter, because if Peter knew *you*, I and everybody else in our immediate world would know about it!"

Just then the elevator door opened and out came the next actress. We hugged good-bye, he said to call him, and I escaped behind the elevator doors, probably totally freaking out the next gal, since it was clear to me she wasn't his type. In the elevator I could hardly compose myself, and when I finally got into my car, all I could do was scream and drive. I couldn't wait to get back to the house and share my experience with Peter and Elaine.

First thing Monday morning, Elaine got a call from the casting director, who said, "There are some people Warren liked, there are some people Warren loved, and then there were those he said he must have in his movie, and Fran falls into the latter category."

Elaine squealed with joy as the guy continued to explain that although I wasn't quite right for the part I'd auditioned for, there was the role of a girl in a bar that both Warren *and* Dustin do a scene with, and *that* would be my part. Girl in bar! Wow-wee, I was thrilled, plus my part of the movie would shoot in New York. What a bonus. We would rehearse for two weeks in New York, then they would leave for Morocco to shoot the bulk of the film before returning to New York to shoot the early scenes of the movie. My God, rehearsing in New York with Elaine May, Warren Beatty, and Dustin Hoffman! How much would any actor pay to be in a workshop situation with these people, and here they were paying *me*!

After I shared the good news with my folks and downed something chocolate, me, Peter, and Elaine powwowed on when would be the appropriate time to call W.B., and Thursday at 10:30 A.M. became the agreed-upon hour.

"Hi, Warren?" I asked the man who answered the phone.

"No, this is his secretary, Andrew. May I ask who's calling and I'll see if Mr. Beatty is in?"

So I told him who I was and that Warren had told me to call, Andrew put me on hold, and I waited . . . then it was Warren Beatty:

"I haven't stopped thinking about you."

What a smooth talker, but I was falling for it hook, line, and sinker. "I hope I'm not calling too early," I said demurely, though still through my adenoids.

If his response was meant to sweep me off my feet, it did.

"You call me any time of the day or night, I don't care if I'm sleeping, eating, or in a meeting, I will take your call."

Now how do you respond to a thing like that? All I could do was giggle. Oy. Then I thanked him for the part and told him how excited I was, to which he suavely responded, "You're very special, we're going to have a good time."

Hmm ... something in that statement made me uneasy, but I quickly dismissed any negative thoughts as a paranoid response to the (literally) dozens of stories that began to rear their ugly heads, told by countless actresses who at one time or another either had had or knew someone who had had a sexual encounter with this insatiable Don Juan de Beatty.

"Do you like paella?" he asked outta nowhere. All I could say was yes. "Great, so why don't you and Peter join me on Sunday for some paella and a screening with friends."

I told him we'd love to but that it really depended on how Peter's father was doing. Unfortunately, his dad was in the final stages of a terminal cancer and was expected to pass away any time now. Then Warren shared the pain he was experiencing from the suffering that his attorney's wife and one of his dearest friends was going through, also from a terminal cancer. He seemed really devastated and so vulnerable that I tried to console him, but what can you say, and took his address and told him I hoped to see him on Sunday. Sadly, Peter's dad passed away on Sunday morning in his own bed, and Peter was there with him in his final hour. I called and canceled out on Warren and didn't see or hear from him again until New York.

I decided to stay with my friend Todd, who owned a beautiful loft apartment in Greenwich Village, and ended up converting the money the movie would have spent on the hotel into a per diem. Now, Todd and I always had a good time together, but now that we had like a thousand bucks a week to blow on just having fun, we were havin' a ball. I would go to a rehearsal hall on South Broadway and work with some of the biggest talents in our industry during the day, and paint the

Todd and me, having a great time spending my "Ishtar" per diem.

town rouge with one of the most brilliant, talented, and funny people I knew (all that was missing was Peter) at night. Needless to say, it was a blast.

The first time I spoke with Warren again was after the first read of the screenplay, when the whole cast sits around a long table with the director and a few other key people and reads the entire movie out loud. Warren waved to me from way across the other end of the table from where I was sitting, along with some of the other lowly actors with small roles (another unknown at the time was Rob Morrow). Afterward, Isabelle Adjani disappeared, and the rest of us mingled.

I don't think Rob Morrow or any of the other actors with lesser parts remained on past that first day, as script changes were constantly being made, but for some reason unknown to me, I, the only three-line part still left in the script, diligently returned day after day to rehearse. Now, you might be wondering what's to rehearse for two weeks with a three-line part? Beats me! Elaine would give us improv situations (all variations of the scene), and we would make stuff up. Maybe they were searching for ideas on what to write in the script, who knows. Mostly I spent my time drinking coffee and observing the masters at work, which was a pleasure.

I became fascinated by Warren's ability to take one hat off and put on another. He would no sooner step out of his character than he would take an important call from Mike Ovitz (the superagent, now president of Disney), or make producing decisions about the movie. Once, during a discussion he was having with the casting director, he called to me to come over. So, of course, I did, at which point he patted his knee and said, "Come sit on my lap."

Now, call me crazy, but I felt embarrassed and somehow like a piece of meat, maybe because the casting guy was in mid-conversation with him, but the request seemed disrespectful to both of us, and I said, "You'll sit on my lap before I'll be sitting on yours."

As if he hadn't heard me, he began to tell the casting director what a brilliant young actress I was while guiding me with his hand onto his lap. Like an idiot, I was bounced on Warren Beatty's lap while he sang my praises to this casting director. Well, as soon as he stopped telling the guy how great I was, you can be sure I got up and marched off, feeling somehow soiled but maintaining my dignity. Warren was the most powerful and openly aggressive man I'd ever met, and I was clearly out of his league when it came to experience. Plus, he was so cute in his baseball cap and sneakers. It was difficult to ever feel like anything but an awkward schoolgirl.

One day Warren asked me if I'd ever met Isabelle Adjani. Well, I hadn't, but was interested in meeting her. She was this beautiful French actress with round cheeks, white porcelain skin, and berry-stained lips. And she seemed mysterious, always off to wardrobe for some costume fitting or hair consultation.

"Well, come with me, she's just down the hall in wardrobe, but I know she'd love to meet you," he said, as if it's the most normal thing in the world that this famous actress from France would ask her famous boyfriend from *Heaven Can Wait* to introduce this unknown girl from Flushing to her, but that's what was happening. Unbeknownst to me, I was being lured into a lion's lair.

As he walked me down the hall he said, "We were both talking about you while lying in bed last night." Huh? Come again? With each step I took I felt myself being transformed into the provincial, awkward, unsophisticated Flushing shlub who lived right beneath the surface of my Hollywood-actress veneer. Just as we approached the door of the wardrobe department, she stepped out as if she were expecting us, wrapped in a turban and layered in traditional Moroccan garb.

"Look who I brought," Warren announced, referring to me.

She extended her hand to me and said, "Warren and I were lying in bed in the hotel last night talking about you." My turn to respond. I figured I'd make casual small talk.

"Oh, what hotel are you staying at? Ya like?"

Warren answered, "I always stay at the Carlton."

Then she continued, "You are very beautiful."

Well, I've always been a maven at chitchat and responded, after clearing my throat because I almost choked on my own saliva, by simply and stupidly saying, "You're pretty, too."

Oh, why can't I be Audrey Hepburn right at this moment, I thought, but life can be cruel, and I was doomed to remain the frog that I am.

Then Warren took over. "We were hoping you would like to join us for dinner this evening, just the three of us . . ."

Now, I don't have to be hit over the head to know what exactly was being proposed. God knows, I hadn't been to Europe, nor did I speak French, but I sure as hell knew a ménage à troiserino when I saw one, and proceeded to stammer and stutter through my response.

"Oh, um . . . that sounds very nice . . . uh . . . but I think . . . no, no, I'm sure I've got . . . I mean, I definitely have plans with my friend Todd, ya know, the guy I'm staying with. Yeah, we have theater tickets, so it's not as if I could cancel, but thanks for asking . . . nice meeting you, Isabelle, honey. Bye!"

And I ran to the bathroom, screaming on the *inside,* "Mommy!" all the way, then sat on the can to compose myself.

News of the movie while on location spread like a cancer throughout Hollywood. The film had major over-budget problems and the whole project became its own *Heaven's Gate*. By the time they all returned from Morocco to New York, some two months later than expected and God knows how many dollars over budget, the decision was made to shoot the bare minimum in New York and leave well enough alone. Needless to say, my part was cut before it was ever shot, and I never saw or heard from Warren Beatty again until years later, when I was promoting *Cadillac Man* on *Late Night with David Letterman* and Warren was selling *Dick Tracy* and opened as a surprise guest.

He jumped into my dressing room, dressed in black, and gave me a hug and a kiss like we had been great old friends. I must admit, he still made my heart flutter. But even years after that, Danny and Donna sat at a table at a fund-raiser with Warren and Annette Bening. Donna told Warren that she was dear friends with Fran Drescher, to which he responded, "We love her, she's so funny on *The Nanny*. We lie in bed and watch her all the time!" Annette and Warren lying in bed, speaking of me . . . Boy, sometimes things sure do come full circle!

Chapter 10

Our House

When we first moved in.

Mom and Dad came out for another visit and were downstairs in the Jacuzzi when suddenly I heard my mother yelling at my father at the top of her lungs, "Leave me alone. I'm not talkin' to you no more, Morty."

Now, my parents *never* fight, so Pete and I couldn't imagine what was wrong. We ran into the living room where the two of them stood, dripping wet.

"What's the matter?" I asked.

My mother, red as a McIntosh, glared at my father, who was stifling a giggle. Dad told us, "Mother is upset 'cause the two ladies sitting with us in the Jacuzzi thought she was my mother."

Suddenly my mother screamed, "No, they didn't, you putz! They only asked you 'cause you keep callin' me *Mother*. I hate that. Don't you ever do that again." My father started to giggle.

"Look at him. Baby Huey over there calling me Mother. I'm not kidding, Morty. I don't want you calling me *Mother* no more! It's fucked up!"

Uh-oh. Ma said the "F" word.

My father turned to stone. "Don't say the 'F' word, babe, I don't like that in front of the kinder [children]."

"What kinder? They're twenty years old. Don't tell ya *Mother* what to do!" Oy, this was getting ugly. My mother started ranting. "The day I turned forty I gave myself permission to say the 'F' word."

Meanwhile, it was all Peter and I could do to stop ourselves from cracking up. We had to think of something.

"Look, why don't we go out to Art's Deli for a triple-decker pastrami?"

"NO! I don't want no pastrami," my mother protested. "I don't wanna do anything. I'm very upset." It was time to pull out the heavy artillery.

"What say we go and look at model homes?"

"No. I don't wanna look at . . . furnished?"

"Yeah, Ma, furnished."

"Well . . ." A long beat. "Let me comb out my hair. Come on, Morty, put on your powder-blue polo shirt. He looks so cute in that."

Whew! Mission accomplished.

Next to life itself, nothing gives my mother more joy than walking through a decorated model home. Well, we fell upon the perfect one. Oh, was it gorgeous. Three levels. Step-up marble tub, big eat-in kitchen, and, yes, a pool. None of us could believe how cheap it was. Something's got to be wrong. We checked, we asked, we discussed, but no, it was just a good deal. So we bought it.

One day we decided to bring Elaine over to get her decorating ideas, and she said, "It doesn't bother you that it's twenty yards from the 101 Freeway?"

Aha! That was it. That's why it was so cheap. But being New Yorkers, noise never bothered us. Believe it or not, we didn't even notice. Well, that was until day after day, night after night, the constant moan of cars, which only let up when there was an accident, or around four in the morning when a lone car would whisk by every few seconds. The only good that came out of it was that my friends would call me to get the up-to-the-minute traffic update.

Well, finally, we could take no more. At this point I was respectfully calling our condo in the valley Amityville. Though the place itself was beautiful, and we were once very happy there, the recession, the L.A. real estate market having dropped out, an unfortunate burglary, and being right across the street from the Ventura Freeway made it nearly impossible to sell even for what we had paid for it some eight years earlier.

One day, it seemed like any other day, we walked out our front door to get the mail and ran into a heavyset guy who said his boss had bought the condo next door, and Peter, without skipping a beat, said that if his boss was interested in our unit, we would sell it cheap. Not because there was anything wrong with it, of course not, we love opening our window to the

Donna and Peter always made a great-looking couple.

drone of cars whizzing by . . . Suddenly I found myself chiming in, explaining that we were actors and wanted to go back to Broadway, the closest to which we had ever come was the twofers TKTS booth in Times Square.

Well, the fat guy chewed on his cigar and thought for a moment, then asked the obvious. "How much?"

Well, we paid 150 plus closing fees, whatever . . . let's say 155. What we didn't know was that his boss was already in escrow on another condo in our development for 185. Needless to say, the guy's broker was on the phone with us by that afternoon, and by the next morning we had sold the condo. Now, as amazing as that sounds, that wasn't even the best part. One day, while scoping the morning papers, I saw a house listed for sale down the road from our friends Danny and Donna, so I called the listed broker and arranged to meet her at the house listed in the classifieds.

Well, it was on their road all right, but right at the part that hangs over the Hollywood Freeway. After that it winds into the hills and becomes beautiful and much pricier. Meanwhile, where was she? I hate this house *and* its location, and on top of everything, she's late. Finally a car pulls up, and she starts right away with the selling:

"Wait till ya see the backyard. It's all"—when I immediately put my hand up, which stops her mid-sentence, but she felt it necessary to complete the sentence anyway—"concrete." I cut to the chase.

"This is nothing like what we want. There is no way I'm ever living so close to a freeway again."

As if she could not comprehend what I was saying she asked blankly, "Don't you want to look inside?"

I apologized for making her come out of her way but declined, and then I said, "Don't you have anything in a nice, quiet neighborhood on a little piece of land with trees? It could be a one bedroom, one bath for all we care, for one-fifty or less?" And if the heavens didn't open up right then when this angel (Merry was her name), this saint, smiled down on me and said that today was my lucky day.

As Peter and I drove up to the address, there it stood. A 1923 pink Spanish bungalow on a quiet, tree-lined street, nestled in a beautiful, old, and well-tended Hollywood community. We parked right in front, a graceful tree spreading its branches across the front lawn, and we rang the bell. The man

Doing my girlfriend Judi's hair for one of her weddings, I forget which. What, too much?

who answered was put off that we were there, but the damned Realtor was late, for a change. We said we'd wait outside, but he grudgingly let us in to take a look around. It was dark and dingy, drab green everywhere, a wheelchair folded in a closet, old carpet covering hardwood floors. I glanced over at this magnificent Romanesque white plaster fireplace and the Moorish vaulted ceilings, the layout, which made perfect sense to me, the old roses bursting with color outside every window. The large square country kitchen even had an oldfashioned laundry room off of it, with a door that opened out to the backyard. I grabbed Peter's arm and whispered, "This is my dream house."

Me and sister Nay being élégante.

When the Realtor arrived, we told her in the bedroom that we wanted to make an offer. She said we would go to her office and write it up just as soon as she showed it to one other family who was just arriving. Oh, swell, again with the waiting? This bitch was getting on my nerves. There we were, leaning against our car, watching this family looking over *my* dream house. During this time, which seemed an eternity, Pete and I decided we would offer the full asking price. Why risk losing it over a few measly grand?

This house was such a fresh listing that it hadn't made the multiple listings yet, nor did it have the FOR SALE sign up. In fact, it had just been handed over to this Realtor the night before. I was sure this family was gonna want it, too. Who wouldn't? Clearly, it was the cheapest house on the block.

Apparently, a crazy old lady had lived in it for some thirty years, neglecting the house and always yelling at the neighbors. Well, when the owner finally died, her two sons decided to price the house so competitively that it would sell fast.

Good, she was saying good-bye to them and walking over to us. "Do they want it, too?" I asked. She said they were going to think about it. Dopes, I thought, and tried to move things along. "Well, let's write it up, shall we?"

The Realtor shifts into automatic and begins to say what a good price the house is at, but she thinks we could probably shave off a few thousand.

"We wanna pay the asking price," Peter proclaimed.

Well, if her jaw didn't drop. What music that must have sounded like to her. But we were nobody's fools, because only an offer of the asking price does the owner have to accept. Well, the offer was made and would be presented to the sons in the morning.

That next morning, I was upstairs wearing an oversized T-shirt and sweat socks, brushing my teeth, when the phone rang. Pete was downstairs playing and singing at the piano, a

The garden. A lot lusher than before.

constant source of joy for him as both the singer and player, as well as for me, the listener. He answered the phone, then called up to me from the bottom of the stairs and said that another Realtor working out of their Century City office had made the same offer that we had, so in fairness to both parties, whoever got to the Hollywood office first to sign the sales agreement would get the house. With a mouthful of toothpaste I said, "What should we do?"

Pete shouted, "Let's go!"

"But I'm not even—"

"Just get in the car."

I didn't even rinse out my mouth.

In a New York minute we jumped in the car and tore ass down the Ventura Freeway and over the hill into Hollywood. Praying that the crosstown traffic was bad, we could conceivably get into Hollywood from the valley faster than our competitor could get from Century City to Hollywood. Well, we arrived, but where was our Realtor? That bimbo, did she ever get anywhere on time? The guy ready to sell to our competition was there with pen in hand, but, alas, he was without a client. We were clients without a Realtor. Who was to enter through the glass door of this tiny, little strip-center mini-mall storefront? Suddenly, and miraculously, the bimbo arrives.

"Where do we sign?" we said as another car pulled into the parking lot outside the office. "Where do we sign?" we yelped at her.

Chester in his garden.

Rutherford in the garden.

The other woman, our competitor, was locking her door and walking toward us.

"Don't you want to hear about the termite contingency?" the bimbo asked.

"No, you'll tell us about it after," we shouted, and we signed the document just as our competitor entered and absorbed the fact that *her* loss was *our* gain. A glorious moment. All we needed was the music from *Rocky*. We still live in our dream house, which is now a sunny country cottage surrounded by a Monet garden. And termites.

Chapter 11

The Snake

Me and my boa.

There is a catalog used in the industry as an aid to casting directors called *The Academy Players Directory.* Actors everywhere pay a nominal fee to ensure that their postage stamp–sized photos be printed among a sea of about two million other photos of like size and category (ingenue, leading lady, character) within this directory. When I started out as an actress, I submitted my picture for the ingenue category. I'll tell ya, the day an actress has to move from the ingenue section over to leading lady is very traumatic. There are some Baby Janes in that ingenue category. It's frightening. They must have used Vaseline Intensive Care as a filter for the camera.

Well, personally, I had never had much luck getting work from this book. But I figured since I was already into eye creams, it was time to say good-bye to the ingenue dream and enter the world of leading ladies.

Year after year, season after season, I diligently submitted my head shot, which also changed with the passing of time. Beginning with perky in gingham, advancing to nymphet in a man's oversized sweater, to sexy but empowered mixed with subtle vulnerability. Well, that did it. That one hit the bull's-eye, and with one telephone call, all those years of paying paid off!

"Honey, ya got a commercial!" Elaine called and said with glee. In those days, small victories were what kept us going.

"What, when, how?" I responded, dumbfounded, since I hadn't been up on anything in weeks, let alone a commercial.

"Are ya ready for this one? They spotted your face in the *Players Directory* and think you'd be perfect for this Charles Jourdan spot. The only thing is"—uh-oh—"ya gotta have a boa around your neck."

"Oh, I like feathers."

"No, honey, not that kind of boa, a boa constrictor. A snake . . ."

"Oh. Well, I like them . . . WHAT??"

Now, if that wasn't strange enough, the commercial would be shot at the home of the producer/director in Cuernavaca, Mexico. Where-navaca? The only place I'd ever been in Mexico was Acapulco, and Peter got sick. Why was all this sounding more like one of those white slavery rings ya read about in cheap romance novels than a legitimate gig? But Elaine said she wouldn't let me go alone and would come, too, if I wanted to do the commercial. Oh, swell, I've seen Elaine in a crisis, she gets the giggles. I can see it all now—I end up somebody's sex slave, complete with a twenty-four-hour hysterically giggling matron. Elaine assured me that everything seemed to be on the up-and-up. The money would be in escrow, and since the live snake wasn't a deterrent, we should absolutely go on this adventure.

So off to Mexico City we went. Upon arrival, we were met by a driver who would take us to Cuernavaca. It was a good hour and a half on dark, winding roads around even darker mountains. It all seemed so ominous. We had no idea what to expect. I tried to track all our moves as time passed and we still weren't anywhere. I mean, I saw that movie of the week where those girls went to Japan as models and singers but wouldn't get their passports back until they'd served six months in a brothel. I looked over at Elaine, who just giggled.

And, of course, the driver spoke no English and didn't seem to comprehend a word of my high school Spanish (which consists of "My name is Fran," "How old are you?" and "Up yours, asshole"), so we were in God's hands. Suddenly I spotted a sign that said BIENVENIDO A CUERNAVACA. Welcome to Cuernavaca. Thank God, we made it. But to where and what? This town was a walled-in city. From the road, all one could see was twelve-foot walls enclosing every property. Was this just the way rich folks lived in Mexico? Or were we entering the sinister world of a drug cartel?

As the massive gates opened like a mouth, we were drawn into an absolute oasis behind high, stucco walls. The property was green and lush, peacocks walked around freely, small, charming cottages dotted the rolling green hills of the beautifully landscaped lawns. It was more gorgeous than Fantasy Island. I felt like screaming, "Da plane, da plane."

The car stopped at the end of a long, winding driveway, and we were greeted by Pablo's wife. Now, the wife was this blond, all-American type who had married this director after having met him while she and a girlfriend were on a holiday in Mexico. She seemed to live a storybook life, taking Spanish lessons each day, taking their children, a beautiful boy and girl, to private school, and assisting her husband in his work. The wife was a photographer and shot stills of all of his jobs. She was very much an American but was already speaking English with a bit of a Spanish accent as she showed us the renovations she was doing on the various guest houses. I guess this was legit. As I gazed upon this glorious Madonna she had encased in an outside wall of their home, I thought, This is the life.

Pablo, the husband and filmmaker, greeted us as we entered their villa. He was a charming man with long gray hair and a mustache, gentle, soft-spoken, and loaded with style. The house was built as a square surrounding an outdoor atrium with covered walkways that connected each room. There were household staff who served platters of food, buffet style, several times a day, and left carafes of fresh water in our rooms each night.

Elaine and I seemed like these loud New Yorkers who had pierced the sanctity of this Mediterranean splendor. But we were in all our glory. When the day came to shoot the Charles Jourdan commercial, two men arrived with bags containing live boa constrictors, each around eight to twelve feet long. I got into makeup, while Elaine, who is petrified of snakes, watched them being unpacked.

"Have those snakes been fed?" I heard her ask one of the snake owners. Apparently they don't bite but kill their prey by squeezing them with their bodies. Oh, well, if they don't bite, I'm not really too concerned, I thought, I mean, if it began to try and choke me, I'm sure someone would cut it off . . .

Meanwhile, for someone who's phobic about snakes, Elaine was taking a perverse interest in the creatures, especially the one that slithered its way down the water fountain that stood

The boa getting stuck in the fountain. They're such little troublemakers.

graciously in the atrium of the house. First two men, then four, then six gathered round to try and pull this snake, merely seeking out a cool, damp spot, from out of the pipes of this fountain. Within seconds it had already managed to find its way into the plumbing, and what suddenly became quite apparent to all of us was that these beasts were solid muscle and not so easy to control. People always ask me what the snake felt like. Well, they're not slimy, not oily at all. I know this may sound crude, but if you've ever felt a man's penis when it's hard, that's exactly what a snake feels like, all wrapped up in the same beautiful, dry, textured snakeskin we make into our wallets, belts, and shoes.

The commercial was to shoot outdoors, near the swimming pool. I wore a tube top, so when the snake began to wind its body around my neck and shoulders I would appear to be nude. I memorized my Spanish dialogue, which would eventually be looped by a real Spanish actress, and sat on a stool awaiting my companion. Elaine and the wife shot roll after roll of film as a twelve-foot boa constrictor seductively wound its way around my neck while I spoke Spanish to the camera. Now, it was quite hot and humid that day in Mexico, and the lights they were using didn't help, so the snake was in constant danger of overheating, which drove Elaine into somewhat shrill and high-pitched giggles. My makeup kept running off and had to be reapplied constantly, but me and the serpent

Me and my boa constrictor in Mexico. Isn't he cute?

persevered. I'll never forget the weight of it, the power, the danger.

Meanwhile, Elaine was so scared she had to lie down. I told her, "Honey, face ya fears. Try it once, and you'll see it's nothing."

"Are you fucking crazy??"

But God love her, she tried it and posed for a picture. There she stood, hysterically giggling, with a huge boa constrictor wrapped around her neck. She was great, then had a double margarita, and passed out. Too bad the photo didn't come with sound.

Elaine with the snake, right before she passed out.

Chapter 12

Cadillac Dog

Chester as a pup.

We dropped into Critterville, the pet store in the Sherman Oaks Galleria, on our way to see a movie at the Cineplex. And there he was. Sitting in the corner of a cage was a red Pomeranian a couple of weeks old. A little ball of fluff.

"Pete, I gotta hold him" is usually my husband's signal to get me out of the store before it's too late, but this time he reluctantly agreed. The salesman handed me the tiny ball of fur, and my son was born.

"Oh, honey, this dog speaks to me. I think I have to have him."

"Baby, having a dog is a big responsibility. We're not ready. Maybe next year."

"Hold him," I said. Peter protested, but I shoved the dog in his arms and the dog licked his face. Oh, this pup is good. He definitely takes after my side of the family. But it didn't work.

Peter said, "No, we can't afford it, it's too much responsibility."

Yada, yada, yada. I left, waving good-bye, and the dog looked at me like "How could you do this to me? Leave the schmuck husband and we'll go live together!" He tore my heart out. Well, what was I going to do, start crying hysterically like a four-year-old? Throw a tantrum and not talk to Peter? Yeah, that sounds good. I waited calmly until the next morning, when suddenly I woke up and started crying.

"I have to have that dog. He's my baby. All my life my parents said when I move out I can get a dog, well, I moved out, I've only one life to live, and I WANNA DOG!"

Oh, if only the Emmy nominations committee had been there then! Finally Peter gave in. We schlepped back to the mall, charge card in hand. And he wasn't cheap. If only it were today, we would have earned enough miles on our card to practically get us to Israel.

The birth of my son.

Chester not feeling well. Playing the martyr. This marked the beginning of his T-shirt obsession.

The salesman pulled him out of his cage, and we decided to call him Chester. "Do you like that, honey?" Oy. Well, he'll bond later. But Pete couldn't help but fall for him, he was so cute, so furry, so small, so quiet. A little doll. That is, until the charge slip cleared. Then all of a sudden, like on cue, Chester started to yap and bark and yap and bark and jump and bark. I told Peter he was just a little excited, he'd calm down. Not to worry. Meanwhile, fifteen years later, he still hasn't calmed down, but I just love him, that's all. I know it's sick, so I won't even mention that I dress him in little T-shirts and he has his own wardrobe.

My first talk-show experience was on *The Pat Sajak Show*. They wanted me to bring Chester on. They thought it was a cute gimmick. The dressing room was on the third floor, through a maze of doors and hallways. So Chester and I waited patiently until we were on. We were a big hit. I sang the song "Tomorrow" from *Annie* with Chester. He did his hula dance trick, we were a fabulous team.

During the commercial break, they brought Chester up to the dressing room to sit with Peter. Meanwhile, the next guest was a classical pianist. He began to play

Chester, when I was giving the baby too much attention.

some sonata, and it was beautiful, but up in the dressing
room, Chester was not happy
that he had so abruptly gotten the hook. So when somebody knocked on the dressing room door to see if
everything was okay, Peter
opened it and Chester ran
out of there like a bat out
of hell, down the stairs,
through the maze of
hallways. He had memorized
the entire way back to the studio.

Is this dog photogenic or what?

Peter yelled after him, "Get back here, Chester. No, no.
Stop."

Thank God, the door to the studio was closed. As Peter
bent down to grab our furry little Dennis the Menace, a cameraman opened the door and Chester ran through the audience, under the piano (and was almost crushed by the man
stomping on his pedals), then jumped across Pat Sajak's lap
and into my arms. The audience howled. I don't think the guy
playing the eighty-eights had a clue as to why. My publicist has
since tried to talk me out of appearing with the little scene
stealer. "Fran, he upstages you," she says. But he's the best five
hundred bucks I ever spent.

Now, according to Elaine's show-biz philosophy, it's better
to be "shit in a hit than a hit in shit," but I always seemed to
be the latter. In fact, one magazine writer once coined me as
being "the actress you can't forget, in movies you can't
remember." I ordered a lifetime subscription to that magazine
after that quote. And *Cadillac Man* did nothing to break the
streak.

I'll never forget how excited I was when Elaine said I was
going to screen-test with Robin Williams for the role of Joy,

one of Robin's girlfriends in the movie. The scene involved an obnoxious little dog, and I thought to myself, Who's a more obnoxious little dog than Chester? Really wanting to get this part, I figured working with a real dog had to make for a better and more animated screen test than, say, a stuffed toy or imaginary dog, and the director agreed, so Chester and I were to test with Robin together.

Every time during the scene when Robin leaned toward me, Chester would growl, and not because he was supposed to, but because he didn't want to share me with Robin. I'm thinkin', This was a lousy idea, there goes my part. But something quite the contrary occurred; the director loved it, and the producer thought it was hysterical. Immediately following the test, the wardrobe woman began taking Chester's measurements and everyone was asking questions pertaining to the little scene stealer. Damn! The dog upstaged me again!

When I called Elaine on my car phone, she asked, "How'd it go, honey?"

I grudgingly admitted, "The audition went great ... for Chester. Watch, he'll get the part but I won't." Then, sounding much like the desperate actress I was, "Tell them Chester doesn't want to work with anybody but me."

I love this shot. They both look great.

Well, fortunately the combo was too wonderful an act to break up, and we were both booked. Elaine grabbed Chester as a client and negotiated his deal. He ended up with (believe it or not) a grand a week and billing above Elaine Stritch! More than I got for my first gig. Everyone took delight in Chester's talent and charisma on the set in Queens, New York, except maybe Tim Robbins, who was quite disgruntled when asked to perform off camera for Chester's close-up. What's the big deal? The dog returned the favor.

"Cadillac Man." The dog's wardrobe came from the children's department at Bergdorf's.

One day the assistant director was searching for Chester to take his position (by this point every-one was regarding him as just another actor on the stage) and questioned me as to his whereabouts. I said I thought he'd stepped out into the parking lot to take a dump, and the guy, in all seriousness, said to me, quite agitated, "Didn't I tell all talent to let me know when they're leaving the set?"

Needless to say, Chester has a way of becoming one of the gang, and it wasn't long before he had his own director's chair, dressing room, and was the recipient of phantom phone messages from Benji in L.A. congratulating him on the movie "Cadillac Dog"!

Well, about four weeks into the shoot, the feedback from the dailies (rough, uncut prints of the previous day's shoot) was that Chester was a star. Meanwhile, I had yet to receive a check on his behalf and decided it was time for his manager, Elaine, to get involved. Elaine was, at this point, smelling a lucrative contract with Alpo, and felt obliged to protect her newest, shortest, and furriest client.

"Chuck [the producer], if you don't cut the dog a check today, the dog walks!" (No one was going to fuck with her client! This rat dog was a potential cash cow.) "Until I receive payment for Chester's services, the dog will not set one *paw* on that stage." (Stranger than fiction is fact.) P.S., the check was cut that day, and Chester (being the devoted son that he is) suggested we use it to remodel the bathroom! He's such a doll.

Then there was our nude scene. Not me and Chester, me and Robin (but Chester was there, too). It was a first for either Robin or me to do a love scene in the nude, but it was in the script and was supposed to be funny.

Meanwhile, the set of a seedy "no-tell" motel must have been 110 degrees, and there was no stopping either of us from perspiring. Now, Billy Crystal once told me his nickname for Robin was Opera Gloves, on account of the fact that he has so much hair on his arms, but nothing prepared me for the amount of fur on this man. Poor Robin was so dear, he kept apologizing for sweating so profusely, but I assured him (while

Judith Hoag, Annabella Sciorra, me, and Lori Petty backstage at "Cadillac Man."

picking his hairs off my body) that he shouldn't be concerned in the least, since in the scene we were supposed to be in the throes of passion anyway. Meanwhile, he was giving new meaning to the title *Gorillas in the Mist.* And to make matters worse, his athletic support kept popping off, which was causing him great anxiety, so I suggested he just pull it off, relax, and let it all hang out . . . and it did. It was a long day had by all.

Chester at the premiere of "Cadillac Man." Before they threw him out for barking.

There was a big premiere for *Cadillac Man,* and we brought Chester, complete with black satin bow tie. We sat in the theater with him, but as soon as the audience started to applaud the credits, Chester barked along with them. Everyone started to laugh at the dog, not at the movie, so Peter thought it best to bring Chester back to the limo for the duration of the film. He was pissed. And left a little present for us in the backseat of the car.

On the Champs-Elysées promoting "Cadillac Man." Oh, honey, this is the life.

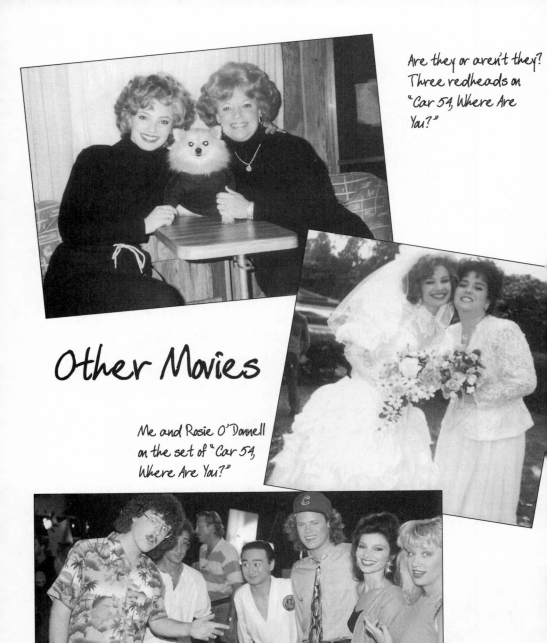

Are they or aren't they? Three redheads on "Car 54, Where Are You?"

Other Movies

Me and Rosie O'Donnell on the set of "Car 54, Where Are You?"

Weird Al, Gedde Watanabe, David Bowe, Victoria Jackson, and me on the set of "UHF."

Chapter 13

Growing Up Is
Hard to Do

By the time I turned thirty, I began to notice that I'd *never* done anything by myself. If Peter had an audition or something, I'd search for another companion to do something with, and if all attempts failed, I'd simply lie in bed and yak on the phone with my mother

Me and Renée Taylor at my thirtieth. Nobody could play my mother better.

Elaine helping me blow out the candles at my surprise thirtieth. She loves this picture. "Oh, honey, I blew it up to poster size."

until Peter'd come home. So all this seemed normal until I began to notice that when I was forced to go out on my own, even for a simple errand, before long I'd begin to get anxious and need to get home. Well, either I was in training to be a guest on *Geraldo,* or this shit's gotta go. So I began seeing Marilyn, the family shrink, who gave me the tools to start enjoying myself by myself (all right, get your mind out of the gutter).

So when my girlfriend Kathryn Ireland Weis invited me to visit her and her family at their country home and vineyard in the south of France (Peter was working on a TV pilot with Dan Aykroyd that Kathryn's husband was directing, and there was no way he could leave), I, after much deliberation, accepted. Now I come from a very provincial middle-class background, where exotic is an umbrella in a frozen drink, so the concept of traveling all the way to Europe on a whim without my husband is about as foreign as eating pastrami with mayonnaise. It just isn't done! But if I wanted to go, it had to be alone. So I valiantly forged ahead, bravely confronting my fears . . . Basically, I'm cashin' in my frequent flier mileage and goin' to France, baby. I'm outta here!

Dan Aykroyd, Peter, and Gary Weis on the set of C.C.P.D.,
   a TV show they produced together for Fox starring Dan.

The car arrived to take me to the airport. Peter and I kissed, we hugged, and I left. As the taxi sped off, Peter yelled, "Wait!"

Oh, isn't that sweet, I thought, as he ran to the cab, flailing his arms. He can't live without me . . .

"Honey, do you know where I put my keys and wallet?"

Well, maybe it was time for separate vacations after all. On my way to the airport, my heart was pounding. Watch, the plane will crash, then I'll be sorry I ever ventured out of my nest. Stop it, I thought to myself, that's crazy talk, "magical thinking," the way Peter's mind works. Oy. Anxiety makes one irrational. Stop thinking this way, I demanded of myself . . . think of Kathryn in France. That's who I will look forward to seeing at the end of this journey through hell. Kathryn, with her beautifully British fifteenth-century classical face. Kathryn, with those enormous breasts, how I can't wait to fall into her bosom and hug her tight. She's a delicious woman, and she is who I will think about.

Believe it or not, I only took one carry-on bag. It went against everything I believe in, but my good friend Donna

Donna and me going to pitch an idea to ABC for a spin-off of "Who's the Boss?" that Peter created. It got made but never sold. Back to the drawing board.

Dixon, a maven of trying to perfect life, advised me once on her secret to packing light. Stick with basic black and roll everything. So I did. I was so cosmopolitan, don't ask. By some miracle (the first of several more to come), TWA was running a frequent flier special, so there I stood in the first-class check-in line at the airport with my twenty-nine-dollar wheely thingamajig, my flowered Ralph Lauren duffel bag, my pocketbook (handbag, to anyone not from Queens), my tickets, my passport, and a pasted-on face of confidence.

"Excuse me, but can I get one of those single seats in first class?" I asked, praying that this jet was one of those models. I mean, the thought of sitting for nine and a half hours with a total stranger would have qualified as beyond torture.

"You're in luck," the TWA agent blurted out after endless pounding on the keypad of her computer. There was only one single seat in first class still not taken. I could have dropped to my knees and thanked Allah right then, but instead I put five dollars in a Salvation Army can and headed toward the terminal.

Once on board, there I sat, conspicuously in the center of the first-class cabin. Pairs of seats on either side aimed like a chevron toward the cockpit, and I felt much like the commander of the starship *Enterprise,* Captain Kirkstein.

Now, when I got on the plane, I looked like shit (well, there's no other way of putting it). Not a stitch of makeup, baggy sweats, and, well, if you added a little vinegar to my hair, you could have tossed a lovely salad. Then suddenly, and without warning, *who* begins putting his carry-on luggage in the overhead storage bin? None other than CBS network president Jeff Sagansky. There he stood, struggling with his hand luggage. That impish grin, an excitement about strong women with star quality, a certain genius mixed with an awkwardness as a man that makes him vulnerable and all the more appealing. When a woman is living in a man's world, as we all are, finding a man who can appreciate, even worship and adore, an empowered woman is truly finding a *civilized* man. Peter is one of those men, and, I believe, so is my CBS president. I said, "Jeff?" He said, "Fran?" I thought, Thank you, Lord, and ran into the bathroom to put on some makeup.

Now, I was just coming off a short-lived CBS sitcom called *Princesses*. The show starred Julie Hagerty, Twiggy Lawson, and yours truly. All the stars got along great. We were relatively happy, or at least Twiggy, me, and Peter were. But there had been trouble in princess paradise, mutual dissent on both the network's and Julie's parts over the basic character she was playing, and after our fifth episode aired we were put on hiatus, otherwise known as "Unemployment opens at eight-thirty on Monday. Be there." Twiggy remained hopeful that we would go back into production after some "retooling" (rewriting, changing, re-casting)

At a photo shoot for "Princesses."
Twiggy was telling me that I
had lipstick on my teeth.

had been done. But I said the night we three got the call, that as sure as I'm standing here, it's OVER! And it was.

Meanwhile, back in the plane, I wondered, What can I do with my hair? Where's that "Pssst" stuff when you need it? A ponytail, that's it. Chic and sophisticated, yet a young and I'm-not-trying-too-hard look. I powdered, I blushed, I painted on a face, but what about that zit? A beauty mark. Hey, it worked for Madonna, but mine looked more like my aunt Ida's mole.

If I didn't think quickly, I might miss this moment. And I've felt the frustration of indulging my insecurity in the moment and then kicking myself repeatedly afterward for not grabbing the brass ring on the merry-go-round. As I stood in the tiny airplane cubicle they call a bathroom, my chest was pounding. And all I kept repeating was "carpe diem, carpe diem," Latin for "seize the day," which I learned by watching the movie *Dead Poets Society*. Now that I looked presentable, I had nine and a half hours to carpe diem him to death. Let's face it, where was he going to go—coach? Oh, baby, this was the "let's do lunch" of a lifetime.

As I opened the door from the bathroom, I saw *him* standing by the stewardess station right next door. All I can say is that this moment can best be described as the moment Dorothy opened the door to a world gone Technicolor.

I sashayed over to him with an air of confidence (wearing my complimentary TWA slipper socks) and asked about the nature of his trip to Paris. Since that's where we were headed, I thought it would be a good opener to a conversation. Apparently, he was off on business. Thank God, I had already been to Paris once before and was able to recommend L'Orangerie, a wonderful restaurant on the Ile-Saint-Louis, and the sculpture gardens of the Musée Rodin, just in casual passing. I don't know if he was interested, or just couldn't believe what French sounded like coming out of my mouth. Thank God, I always had a taste for travel and living beyond my means. It sure helps you hold up your end of the conversation during cocktail parties with kings. Well, it was paying off for me now.

I tossed out a line with bait and he bit. A man after my own heart. A traveler. We chatted about the wonderful Relais & Châteaux (a very exclusive, very discriminating membership of privately owned small inns and hotels around the world) hotels that dotted the California coastline and great restaurants in New York and Los Angeles. Boy, were we ever connecting. I must say, I can talk to anyone about anything in limited quantities, ya know, just as the well runs dry on a particular subject, just reach down and grab some nuts (Planters, not Jeff's) and change the subject. That's good cocktail conversation.

We stood at that stewardess station for what seemed like hours. God, the names I dropped, the places I described. I bet he never guessed I was in first class on a frequent flier special (although the seven little bottles of Baileys stuffed in my purse might have given me away . . . Well, I didn't want to arrive at Kathryn's empty-handed). But enough about travel, let's talk about me . . .

"Ya know I've got a development deal with you over at CBS?" He boyishly answered, "I know," but I somehow was surprised that he knew, Jeff seemed too important to know. But that's what was so amazing about him, he seemed to know everything. As I leaned against the coffee counter I listened to him as he went on about my character in *Princesses* not doing me justice, only showing a single facet of my larger-than-life per-

The pilot of "Princesses." Twiggy, me, and Julie Hagerty. We all had such high hopes, but it wasn't meant to be.

sonality. God, he sounded like Peter. This guy really gets what I'm about.

Since the unfortunate failure of *Princesses*, my determination to become a producer had only increased. If I must suffer by mistakes made, at least let them be *my* mistakes, *that* I can live with. Or at least obsess about. And I told Peter, in so many words, "If we don't get on the inside soon, I'm packin' it up and movin' to Massachusetts!" And from that moment on, we began brainstorming new show concepts of our own for me to star in.

There Jeff stood, going on about how many scripts were on order for the next pilot season and how "we've" got to find something that does me justice. Talk about chutzpah, but suddenly I found myself pitching an idea. Hey, as the Talmud says, "If not I, who?" and "If not now, when?" (or something like that).

"Jeff, no one understands my character as well as me and Peter. We've been analyzing it for years, and no script comin' down the pike is gonna fit me hand in glove like ours can." I felt so empowered. (With that, a bottle of Baileys fell out of my purse, which I discreetly kicked down to coach.) "We've studied sitcoms through TV viewing and personal experience as actors for years, not to mention that Peter's now writing and producing full-time." I had an answer for everything. I truly believe the angels were guiding me. I was experiencing a moment when life was in perfect harmony. I felt us really connecting as he just nodded, then grabbed the stewardess for a scotch.

Eventually they announced that the movie was about to begin. Barbra Streisand in *The Prince of Tides*. His "favorite movie," he proclaimed, and I silently blessed him for that, followed by an oral blurt of "But ya gotta promise me you'll hear our pitches for my next show when we get back to L.A. . . . ." He agreed as we both returned to our seats and the lights began to dim. On the outside I was cool as I fitted on my headset, but inside I was the commercial of the caged chimpanzee bouncing off the walls with a piece of Samsonite luggage. Meanwhile, Barbra looks gorgeous in this film. I wonder if she's had any work done? Anyway, talk about being in the right plane at the right time . . .

As we deboarded the plane at the Charles de Gaulle Airport, Jeff's last words were, "When we both get back to L.A., call me and I'll set up an appointment to hear your pitch." Boy, you can stay home waitin' for the phone to ring or you can throw yourself into life, it's always a wonderful surprise what ya bring back. I couldn't wait to call Peter, my heart was palpitating.

Meanwhile, ya need a Berlitz course just to figure out the French pay phone. "Honey, honey, I'm at the Paris airport and guess who was on the plane coming over with me?"

"Cher?" he answers, without skipping a beat.

"NO!!" (Look how he goes right to Cher, she should only know how my husband has the hots for her.) "Jeff Sagansky. Jeff Sagansky was on my plane!"

I filled him in on everything and was so high that I didn't even care that all by myself I now first had to find "le tram bleu" to take me to "terminal trois." That meeting with Jeff justified the entire trip, and now I could enjoy it guilt-free. I felt like I'd just walked across burning-hot coals, I felt invincible . . . vive la France!

Chapter 14

On the Vineyard

Oui, oui.

Oy, was that lousy tram ever crowded, and everyone smoked. Not to mention, hasn't anybody here heard of Right Guard? Thank God, it was a short flight. And then, like a mirage, I stood in the terminal at the Toulouse airport and caught my first glimpse of Kathryn as she stood with her older boy, Oscar. An adorable but very precocious three-year-old.

I threw down my bags and flung myself into her arms like a long-lost lover, and in that moment Oscar began tugging at Kathryn's blouse, whining repeatedly, "MAMA, I'M TIRED, MAMA, I'M TIRED."

That was the beginning of Oscar's plot to destroy my trip to Toulouse. She praised me on what little baggage I carried. I replied, "Oh, honey, I always travel like this." She loaded up the Audi and we were off to the vineyard in Verlhac Tescou, France.

On the freeway I start to tell Kathryn about this amazing coincidence of meeting Sagansky on the plane, when suddenly and shrilly from the backseat a plastic cup hits my head and Oscar shouts, "I WANT BANANA, MAMA, I WANT BANANA." She calmly offers him some "lovely blueberries" instead. That quieted him down long enough for me to explain exactly who Jeff was and how important a position he held at the network, when again from the backseat, "BANANA, MAMA, I WANT BANANA," and I'm thinking, Does this kid say *everything* twice? I throw him a banana from the grocery bag Kathryn wedged between my legs.

"Here, here's your banana, eat it in good health," I said with a clenched smile, and then shifted gears to resume back to me.

Suddenly I looked down at my feet and realized that with all the excitement, I was still wearing my TWA slippers, when "STRAWBERRIES, MAMA, I WANT STRAWBERRIES." Again with the fruit? Boy, this kid really likes fruit. I wouldn't want to have to change his diapers.

Kathryn reaches into the bag, totally controlled by the little monster, I mean, Oscar, and responds lovingly, "Does my puppy want *framboise*? Say *framboise*, darling. *Framboise*," and passes him some strawberries, when I, already nervous and thinking, although I've never tried one, I know I'm in need of a martini, ask in a controlled tone, "How long before we get there?" And as the Audi speeds off into the horizon, Kathryn cheerfully says, "Not far, darling, just an hour and a half or so."

"FRAMBOISE, MAMA, I WANT FRAMBOISE . . ." Oy.

Well, fifteen pounds later, I happily settled into life on the farm. The vineyard was surrounded by beautiful fields of sunflowers, and the view of the hillsides from the house was a patchwork of yellows and browns. Kathryn, who owns and operates Ireland Pays, a chi-chi decorating shop in Santa Monica, has such great taste, it was like living in a page right outta *Elle Decor*. The afterglow of a setting sun shone in a purple sky till nearly 10:00 P.M., when we'd first be going in to prepare a pasta and salad supper. We'd eat on the patio by the light of a single flickering flame and the scent of citronella, while the French mosquitoes nipped at my ankles. They can be so rude!

I am officially at the stuffed-sausage stage and still eatin' strong. God bless the person who invented the elastic waistband. The goose farmer dropped off a dozen jars of pâté, triple crème blue cheese (not even in the same stratosphere with the crap I've been eatin'), and a batch of homemade saucisson sec, ya know,

Kathryn Weis, Oscar, and Otis on the infamous trip to France.

for a snack. The housekeeper would drive up the gravel road that led to the house with white bakery bags filled with chocolate croissants (the chocolate was still melty inside from having been freshly baked). And the wine was free-flowing. After all, we *were*

I was trying to relax when Oscar decided to use my hammock as a swing.

on a vineyard. Kat would say, "Red, white, or rosé?" at lunchtime, and would keep asking till the stars came out. Oh, it was all so decadent and delicious.

Each morning I'd be awakened by the shrill scream of either Oscar, whom by now we were both calling Dennis the Menace, or baby Otis, who would only start to cry the moment Oscar finally stopped. But it wasn't entirely their fault, the kids had nothing to amuse themselves with. Haven't these people ever heard of a TV? A VCR? *The Little Mermaid?*

I remember an afternoon when the boys were in particularly rare form, and in a desperate attempt to save the day, Kathryn suggested we all go to the next village, where there was some kind of a kids' train ride the boys could go on. "They always have so much fun when they can scream their heads off," she said enthusiastically.

"Oh, gee, that sounds like unbelievable fun, but you really need to have your quality time with just you and the boys . . . alone." I think I'd rather stay home and have a hysterectomy.

Me, the hippies, and a lush named Oscar.

I watched as a cloud of dust kicked up from the tires of the little Audi as she, her two boys, and the Guatemalan nanny drove off to the next village, a banana peel flying out the rear window. I quickly and desperately dialed Peter in L.A. Having never actually *lived* with children, this introduction was more like a hazing, and I wept pitifully on the phone. Peter calmed me down and said that Twiggy had called and invited me to visit them in London. Twiggy? Twiggy with the quiet, non-fruit-eating, teenaged kids? But that would mean changing my tickets, traveling through more airports in other countries, maybe I was making too much of this. With that, I reached behind my back and pulled off a lollipop stuck to my sweater. Or not.

It was dinner that night with the hippies from Scotland that helped me make up my mind. These young, wonderfully free, pot-smoking, brown-toothed travelers turned life into one big adventure. I sat outside under the stars with them, fascinated. I'd never met people like this in Flushing, I can tell you that much. True travelers, no cares or responsibilities, no fears, just the outstretched road that lay ahead and more days

Van Gogh, eat your heart out.

like this one. Yes, I will journey to London. I will take the adventure, I will be like my friends the Scottish hippies. P.S., Oscar was getting inebriated on sips of wine he stole from everyone's glass, which only I seemed to notice, being the neurotic Jew that I am. Meanwhile, the poor kid was getting schnockered. But, actually, he made a very happy drunk, quite the life of the party. Well, I guess this *was* sorta my bon voyage party . . .

Chapter 15

Lucky England, When It Rains It Pours

Ace, Leigh, Twiggy, and Carly.

Boy, I'm really living on the razor's edge now, I thought to myself as the limo dropped me off in front of Twiggy's house. Hardly the type of adventure the hippies might have taken, but pretty damned aggressive for a little girl from Queens whose only thing she ever did alone was take a shit, and even that was with the door open!

Bravely I rang their bell, just praying they'd be home (I mean, they were expecting me, but you never know with these Europeans). Thank God, they buzzed me in. I'm here, they're home, boy, I'm travelin' now! Twiggy and Leigh Lawson— Peter and I always called them the Charmings, because they are. We love them, they are truly delightful people. And she's an absolute icon, yet as down-to-earth and regular a person as you'd ever want to meet, with a teenaged daughter, Carly, who is truly one of the most wonderful and talented young people I know. And Leigh, a talented actor unto himself, can you believe, who, before Twigs (yes, she's still a stick), was married to Hayley (*The Parent Trap*) Mills? Isn't that wild? Two of the most famous Englishwomen I grew up wanting to be (or at least sound like). He and Hayley had a beautiful son who's nicknamed Ace, and who always calls Twiggy by her real name, Leslie. This is so great.

Leigh Lawson, the inspiration for Mr. Sheffield.

The longer I stayed with this wonderful British family in this large rambling apartment (or flat, as they call it in Europa!), the more shlubby I became. I'd never felt so close to Flushing as when I stayed with them in London. Was I always so loud and crude? Don't answer that. I

Ace and Carly, Twiggy and Leigh's children. The beginning of "The Nanny."

was like a bull in a china shop. Wave a red scarf, I might have stampeded. I schlepped Carly all over town, the poor thing wore her new shoes and complained about blisters. But I showed no mercy. I was going to see London come hell or high water and, slipping a bit into my old ways, preferred *not* to do it alone, so I simply told her, "Honey, just walk on the backs of your shoes."

"Won't that break them?" she questioned, to which I quickly responded, "No, no. Break them *in*."

And that was the beginning of *The Nanny*.

Twiggy, myself, and Carly, the
inspiration for "The Nanny."

Chapter 16

Back in La La Land

"It's kinda a spin on *The Sound of Music,* only instead of Julie Andrews, I come to the door" is what I said to Peter, who always had a sixth sense for this stuff.

He took a beat and said, "That could be it, we'll develop it as soon as you get home." Three weeks later I was wondering what to wear to the network.

As I gazed in my closet, scanning my wardrobe, there I stood, a good fifteen pounds overweight. Forget pants, or anything short, move into the long skirts and dresses. The crème brûlée and chocolate mousse section. I took a flashlight and searched through the sea of black, and found a long dress that hid a multitude of sausage, I mean, sins. A pair of high-heeled Manolo Blahnik mules (when you feel wide, add height) completed the look. If there's one thing my mother taught me through example, no matter how heavy you happen to be, sell it to the world as voluptuous, with confidence and no apologies, and the world will respond as such (except for those few nonbelievers who'll call ya a fat ass behind your back). So I set my hair, put on makeup, and swept into CBS with Peter like I was the greatest, most glamorous star there ever was. The receptionist welcomed me and complimented me on how gorgeous I looked. It's working, I thought to myself. And secretly blessed her.

Every important exec over at CBS seemed to pass through the waiting area where we sat. Jeff Sagansky charged out of the elevators and headed toward his office. I yelped "Jeff" in my usual nasal drone; that stopped him dead in his tracks. I slid off the oversized couch (I prayed everyone realized that that embarrassing sound was coming from the faux leather, not me), ran over to say hello and give him a peck on the cheek (well, after all, we had spent nine and a half hours together; by L.A. standards we were practically engaged), and introduced him to Peter. "Ya know, we're about to meet Tim Flack"—at the time, the head of comedy development at CBS—"with our idea."

"Good luck, I hope it goes well."

Now, this is the way my mind works: He seemed so much nicer on the plane, and now much cooler and more businesslike, what, was he just using me, treating me like an equal when he had nobody else and now I'm back to being a peon? Somehow I felt like a jilted lover, but decided not to take it personally, since he might have a thing or two else on his mind, being the president of the network and all. With that, the receptionist sent us into Tim's office, and Jeff was gone like a flash down the corridor. Nothing left but the scent of his Aramis.

Tim, who has since died of AIDS, was a fabulous and flamboyant man unlike most you'll usually meet within the corporate structure of a network. Peter and I marched into Tim's beautiful office. He was always into externals. I'll never forget one time when Elaine and I were yapping on the phone, anxiously awaiting a call from Tim regarding some delicate negotiations on a project I was wanted for, when she suddenly said, "Honey, I'll call ya back, that's Tim on the other line, this could be it!" Ten minutes later she called me back.

"Well, what did he say? Do we have a deal?" I asked with the kind of desperation you have when you're thirty thousand in the red and every charge is maxed!

"Honey, he was calling to find out *who* did Donna Dixon's wallpaper in *Architectural Digest*."

Nu? That was Tim, but ya had to love him. There Tim sat with Joe Voci, the director of comedy development, waiting for us to blow them away, or maybe the whole meeting was a "mercy fuck," as Elaine calls meetings that are more of a favor or a jerk-off. Well, we were gonna give it our best shot come hell or high water.

Peter starts with, "It's called 'The Nanny.' A door-to-door cosmetics girl from Queens selling 'Shades of the Orient Cosmetics'"—whatever that is, but it sounded funny—"knocks on the door of a wealthy English widower with kids, a butler, and an ice princess business partner, in desperate need of a nanny, who mistakes Fran for an applicant, and Fran gets the job! Sort of like a fish out of water."

Then I chime in, "Or as I like to call it, a gefilte fish out of water." Oy, did I just say that? I think to myself.

Then Peter grabs the reins again. "Fran scribbles a resumé with lipstick on an order form from her cosmetics case and hands it to Mr. Sheffield, who begins to read it, somewhat impressed that she apparently worked for the Queen Mother. Fran corrects him, saying, 'No, silly, that's not the Queen Mother, that's my mother from Queens.'"

Tim and Joe burst into laughter. We hooked a fish. Tim asks, "What does Mr. Sheffield do for a living?"

I say, "Well, he's very wealthy, old money, you know. I imagine he busies himself with real estate, stock holdings, that sort of thing . . ." No comment.

Then Peter, whom I like to think of as the new Golden Boy of television, says, "Ya know, I was kinda toying with the idea of Mr. Sheffield and his partner being Broadway producers."

And I'm thinking, What the hell does blue collar meets blue blood have to do with a Broadway producer? when suddenly Tim squeals, "I love it," followed by an equally enthusiastic squeal from Joe, saying, "I love it, too" (network executives tend to respond to things in order of position and rank), at which point I could have given Peter a blow job right there on the spot, but chose to squeal, "I love it three!" Oy.

Peter handed them a breakdown of the concept and the characters, which they were delighted to receive. Apparently, most writers do a verbal pitch on their ideas and don't leave anything floating around to be read by God knows who and risk getting a winning idea ripped off by the wrong person. We've since stopped trying to be so helpful at these meetings and now do verbal pitches like all the other paranoid Writers Guild of America members.

"What's the next step?" I asked. Elaine always said never leave a meeting without driving it into the next step, so we don't.

Tim responded, "I'm going to pitch 'The Nanny' to Jeff [Sagansky]."

Then Joe chimed in, "You'll hear in a few days," and we were excused. If I was a cartoon, my heart would have been pounding out of my thorax! A few weeks went by. We hadn't heard a thing. Oh, well, it's no big deal. It was fun while it lasted. Meanwhile, hide the razor blades. But wait . . . back at CBS a call was being placed . . .

Tim pitched the idea to Jeff in one simple sentence: "Fran Drescher is the nanny from hell," and Jeff loved it.

Joe called Peter and me with the news like a delivery nurse

who announces the birth to the pacing father in the waiting room. He exclaimed, "It's a green light."

Oh, my God. It wasn't over after all. Hooray! Pass out the cigars, it's a green light. What the hell is a green light? Joe went on to explain that he was ordering a script. Call everyone, shout it from the mountain tops, Peter and I conceived a green light. (To this day we refer to *The Nanny* as our baby, and I'm the cash cow that feeds it.) So what's the next step? We needed a studio and experienced executive television producers to supervise.

We read a lot of scripts, but Rob Sternin and Pru Fraser of Ink, Inc., were most in sync with our writing style. We've always enjoyed their TV shows in the past (*Who's the Boss?*, *The Charmings*, and *Married People*) and felt that they just might be the ones to share in the raising of our kid. Now, it's funny how things sometimes fall into place. Coincidentally, Rob and Pru took a meeting over at CBS to pitch an idea of their own for Fran Drescher. Well, CBS explained that they were already committed to doing *The Nanny* for me but that they (Rob and Pru) would also be good for that project as well!

Rob Sternin and Pru Fraser, our partners in crime.

Boy, I'll tell ya, after fifteen years of near hits but mostly misses, it's sometimes hard to believe it when you're actually *in* the game. A contender, a player. But there we were, two kids from Flushing, interviewing executive producers and studios for *our* TV show that *I* would star in . . . Well, I'm getting a little ahead of myself because when it was all said and done, there were many hurdles yet to jump. So a meeting was set for

Rob and Pru at the same time that Peter was talking to the studios.

His first meeting was at TriStar Television. Now, Jon Feltheimer, the president of both Columbia and TriStar Television, was once an actor who had actually worked with Peter in a Freshen-Up gum commercial a decade and a half earlier. How's that for a small world? Wait. It gets smaller. They suggested an executive producing team who happened to be married, and Peter immediately interrupted and said, "Is it Rob and Pru?" And the answer was YES.

Boy, if the meeting with this Rob and Pru goes well, it looks like we've got show runners (executive producers) and a studio. Well, there was an instant connection. They were a

Peter played a nerd in the Freshen-Up commercial with Jon Feltheimer.

married couple like us, together since college. She's a gentile from Texas, he's Jewish and from Long Island. They seemed casual and easy to be around. They even argued about something in front of us like a real married couple. I love that. They're normal. So we went with Rob and Pru, and TriStar, and this is where our fantastic voyage begins . . .

Years later, this picture was stuck on my refrigerator to remind me that I'm a person with a weight problem.

Chapter 17

This Little Piggy . . .

Well, ya know, the camera puts on ten extra pounds, and I already had fifteen to lose, so first order of business, lose twenty-five big ones. I must say, losing weight is somewhat easier when you've got a deadline. Be it a vacation, a wedding, or, in my case, a TV pilot.

So I was off to an exercise class. Uh-oh. Try huffing and puffing your way through an hour class alongside the likes of Annette Bening (who's a stick), Shalom Harlow (a supermodel, need I say more?), Lesley Ann Warren (thin thighs, big tits). Thank God, Donna Dixon was several months pregnant or I really would have slit my wrists! But my Weight Watchers meeting was always a safe haven, besides, I was one of the thinner ones there. And if L.A. is good for anything, it's a great place to get on a health kick—there are more people compressed into one region trying to discover the fountain of youth than I've found anywhere else in the world. Everywhere you look there's a juice bar, a gym, fat-free yogurt shops, not to mention all the Hollywood wanna-bes. The beautiful people jogging, working out, swimming, and running from one support group to another between unemployment and tanning salon appointments. Well, when in Rome . . . Before long I was one of those people doing my errands in my leotards and Nikes, sipping nonfat mocha lattés, discovering the joys of Pilates (the exercise du jour).

Now, to have grown up in my family, it seemed life was about eating and dieting, well, eating and talking about dieting. My dad was born the day the stock market crashed, October 29, 1929, which profoundly shaped his attitudes to many things, but food certainly is at the top of the list. "Waste not, want not" and "Take all you can eat . . . eat all that you take!" The poor guy spent the better part of his adult life finishing what others left on their plates just so he wouldn't endure the guilt of throwing out food.

Our first big vacation, to San Diego. At this point, my sister was called the thin one.

The first sign of an eating disorder is when you take pride in the fact that you have the hugest appetite of anyone. When your family brags to others (as mine did) that their daughter can eat

Kishkalas. Like mother, like daughter.

all the men under the table, let this be a sure-fire indicator—
you have a problem. How anyone can be thrilled at the
prospect of eating more than anyone else is beyond me, and yet
there was a time when I was. Peter and I used to order three
entrées. One for him, one for me, and one so we wouldn't
starve.

I shouldn't tack this all on my father, though, because
believe me when I tell you that my mother has her own accel-
erated mishegas with food. I have never seen a person get so
genuinely joyful as Sylvia when she's feeding someone.
Anyone! It could be fish in an aquarium, the woman has an
orgasm. Age four was the last time in my life I was slim without really trying. Then the old Jewish concern that I was *too*
thin became a permanent concern throughout the family, and
the campaign began to fatten me up. "What should we do, call
the doctor? She's too thin."

Each day my mother and I would walk my sister to kinder-
garten, followed by a walk to the corner luncheonette for an
egg cream and a sugar daddy (a milk, chocolate syrup, and
seltzer drink, and a large caramel lollipop), per the doctor's

Peter and me in "Once Upon a Mattress" at Hillcrest High School. Too much makeup? Nah. When I saw this picture, I went on a diet and lost thirty pounds.

orders. My mother would sit and kvell, "Eat, mamalah, it makes me so happy." She'd sit and stare at me so gleefully, I didn't have a prayer, and by second or third grade I was already aware of the fact that there were other little girls who were much thinner than I, ate less than I, and had thighs that weren't intimate friends (Amy Semel and Dori Erdman, both baring toothpick legs, come to mind). By fourth grade I was already wearing black.

I remember that I never enjoyed going to other children's homes for dinner because the portions were always too small. I'd come home depressed. It never occurred to me that my appetite was too big. I was fed when I was sad, I was fed when I was good, we ate to celebrate, we ate to mourn. And in between, we'd discuss what we were going to eat later. The only thing they never did with food was deny it as a punishment. Oh, no, that would have been too cruel and unusual. I mean, my parents are people who walk off dinner by taking a fifty-foot stroll over to Baskin-Robbins.

Those who watch me on *The Nanny* would never believe that in high school I actually peaked at around 150 pounds, but I did. In those days, Peter, who was six feet tall, weighed less than I did, and I was only five five. But by my senior year I

Me, Marilyn the
shrink
and Peter.

knew I wanted to
become a professional actress and
was determined to lose weight. Of course, at seventeen, smoking cigarettes and starving seemed like a good way
to go about it, and I managed to reduce down to a svelte 115
pounds. What I still hadn't realized yet was that I had merely
replaced one extreme eating disorder with another, resulting in
a yo-yo pattern that would continue for years. Oh, is this
depressing. What's in the fridge? (Only kidding . . .)

Vacations were one time when I could rationalize going on
a binge. Going away and having a good time meant eating
everything in sight and returning at least ten pounds heavier.
Then you knew you'd had a good time. Oh, and there were
those holidays defined by an eating orgy (i.e., Thanksgiving,
Christmas, Passover, Pass It to Me, Pass Me Some More . . .).

All I can say is, God bless Weight Watchers, Marilyn (my
therapist), and Marilu Henner for contributing to the change
in my thinking about food. All my life, I would choose what I
ordered from a menu not necessarily by what I was in the
mood for, but by how large I thought the portion would be.
Consequently, I rarely if ever ordered shrimp, because ya never
get enough. Pretty sick, huh? Peter and I still joke about a
brunch we went to with my parents. When the waitress (who

my dad was already playing up to in an attempt to get on her good side) requested the dessert orders, my dad could not make up his mind until the waitress answered his ill-fated question, "Is the cheesecake precut?" To which her response was yes. (Uh-oh, that means cut into even, small pieces. Even if I play up to her, she won't be able to cut me an extra-big piece.) Needless to say, Morty was not gettin' the cheesecake at that brunch! My mom once questioned whether the air-popped popcorn she was snacking on, although fat-free, was keeping her from losing more weight. I asked how much of it she was eating and she replied, "I eat till I get nauseous and then I stop . . . usually."

I thank Weight Watchers for giving me the key to freedom. And now, although I still enjoy and appreciate food, I eat to live, no longer do I live to eat. But if I slip at a meal and fall off the wagon, I forgive myself, as I am only human, and get right back on track rather than allowing it to turn into a three-day binge. I also tend to order two other beverages (water and tea), along with a glass of wine, taking sips from each in order to stretch the single glass of wine throughout the meal. I never put butter on bread anymore, and I tend to eat the crust and leave the middle. I request dressings on the side, light on the oil during food preparation, and limit my red meat consumption to once in a great while, fish and skinless chicken to a few times a week (a portion the size of an audiocassette), and round out my meals with large amounts of pastas, grains, and vegetables. I eat three times a day, never allowing myself to get so hungry that I make the wrong choices. I sound like I got it all figured out, but believe me, I screw up plenty.

For a long while, eating this way seemed to be all the breakthrough I needed to maintain a slim physique until I befriended Marilu Henner, the actress, that is . . . Over a dinner at our house, Marilu began to tell us about her miracle diet. I had to comment on how great she looked so soon after giving birth. Meanwhile, my cousin claims she's still holding on to some residual post-pregnancy weight and bloat, and her kid just got bar mitzvahed. But there Marilu sat, chattering away in tight, black jeans, a ball of energy with a clear and beautiful complexion, and proceeded to tell us that she had eliminated all dairy from her diet. That means *all* milk and milk by-products from any animal forever! No cheese? Oh, this is way too radical for me, I thought, as I shoved a piece of mozzarella in my mouth. I glanced over at Howie, our other dinner guest and dear friend, who also lives to eat and did not seem to be coming up for air any time soon. This was not the group from which to find new recruits.

"If you want to see weight drop off, have boundless energy, a faster metabolic rate, and reduce significantly any allergies you might be suffering from, you'll try it, and within six months you won't believe the change," she pontificated.

My only response was, "Not even Parmesan on pasta?"

"You can get a substitute Parmesan made of soy!" she answered with a straight face.

Here I was, finally making enough money to buy the imported kind, and she's pushin' a substitute? Ehh, I chalked the whole thing off to some fanatical Hollywood fad as I digested my favorite fat-free ice cream and made Howie a mocha latte.

It wasn't until Peter and I ventured to Martha's Vineyard a few months later that I decided to try Marilu's program. As we flew from New York to the Vineyard on the company jet so generously offered to us by Mickey Schulhof, the president and CEO of Sony Corporation of America at the time (I'll tell ya, it's nice to be on a hit series), I said to Peter with conviction, "While on this trip I'm not going to have anything rich or fattening, definitely *no* New England clam chowder just swimming in that heavy cream and butter!"

Wouldn't ya know it, our first meal Peter said to the waitress, "I'll have the New England clam chowder," and without skipping a beat I heard myself saying, "And I'll have one, too! Make it a bowl!"

Needless to say, as we waddled back on the plane four days

Me and Pete in Nantucket, doing our best to look Waspy.

later feeling like two beached whales, Peter suggested that we go on a fast, but since it was dairy that we'd OD'd on, I brought up the Marilu program. Well, we started it right there on the plane, and I've been happily dairy-free ever since. P.S., it's everything she claimed it would be and then some. My skin got thinner, my face got clearer, and much to my relief, I don't crave cheese. I compare cheese to chocolate. When you eat it, you crave more of it, and when you stop eating it, you stop craving it. Believe me, I've got nothing against dairy, per se. Everyone's body is different.

Plus, eliminating dairy automatically cuts out a shitload of evils like rich desserts and cream sauces, but the best boner of all is that it's virtually impossible to cheat on this program because the minute you try and reintroduce that sinfully rich whipped-cream cake (even just a bite) back into your diet, your body reacts with a major allergy attack. I'm talking stuffed nose, watery eyes, sneezing, you name it. This I can

compare to quitting smoking. Even though your body toler-
ated cigarette smoking for years, after you've quit and then
bum one at a party, you feel instantly dizzy, nauseated, and
headachy and generally feel like shit. Only with dairy, the negative reaction is even better (I mean worse), because you blow
all your makeup off and look like shit, too! Today I am finally
liberated from a lifetime of yo-yo dieting by a healthy eating
lifestyle and am now finally what that four-year-old me was
intended to be. At long last!

*My parents and me in Nantucket.
What a wonderful place!*

Chapter 18

Putting It Together

I'm now down twelve pounds and am reminded of a quote from Gene Tierney when asked what she remembered most about her career: "I was always hungry." P.S., *she* suffered a massive break-down. Oy. Meanwhile, I was like a horse with blinders on, focused only on two things: losing weight and writing the pilot script.

Now, we were all going along our merry way *thinking* we were making a pilot (a pilot is, essentially, the first episode of the series that tells the story of how all the characters come together) until we were told we weren't. But wait, if we're not making a pilot, what the hell are we doin' here? Apparently, in an effort to save money, the network was only kicking in enough moolah to produce a fifteen-minute synopsis. This way, in case it stinks, if they spend less, they lose less.

Peter and me,
the first day in our new office.

Since there was really no choice in the matter, we took what money we could get. But Rob and Pru very wisely insisted we produce the whole half-hour teleplay and just cut corners wherever we could.

Rob said, "I've never had a presentation that got a pickup, and I've never had a pilot that didn't . . . let them finance it the way they want, but we're making a pilot!"

And we did. By that time, Rob and Pru seemed to really love and believe in *The Nanny,* and we loved them for that. The whole event took on the scope of a Mickey Rooney/Judy Garland movie. Every person brought on board took delight in the zeal, freshness, and positive energy of the making of *The Nanny.*

We brought set pieces in from canceled shows all over town. If you look carefully, you'll notice that the set in the pilot episode differs significantly from the set you see on all subsequent episodes. Our kitchen came from the movie *Lost in Yonkers* (which we kept, but I would still like to repaint someday), the living room was actually from *Sibs,* and the staircase was a leftover from *Leave It to Beaver.* When the show got

Fittings for the gown in the pilot.

picked up, we had a proper budget to build the Sheffield mansion the way we had always envisioned it. Well, who's kidding whom, there is always a budget to contend with, and rather than build, we opted to use the staircase from *The Powers That Be*. But that, we loved. It had a *Beverly Hillbillies* thing going for it.

Even when it came time to design "the Nanny's" look, which we all agreed should make a real fashion statement, we had to beg, borrow, and steal. We hired Brenda Cooper (whom I worked with on *Princesses*) to do the costumes. She pulled garments from her closet, my closet, her sister's closet (I still don't think she knows, uh-oh, now she does . . .), as well as the studio wardrobe department and every sale rack in town, in the end creating the look that would bring glamour back to eight o'clock TV. It seems nowadays that I'm as well known for the clothes I wear as I am for my voice.

But this reputation for style didn't happen overnight, and could not have been achieved without the early support of

Brenda "dahling" Cooper, our Emmy award-winning costume designer.

My fitting for the famous "Lady in Red" dress.

generous designers such as Todd Oldham and Gianfranco Ferré. The most expensive gown I wore was in the Streisand episode: a $15,000 Bob Mackie (or at least that's what he charged the Oscars the night Madonna wore it in a number). We, however, rented it, and gingerly returned it the next day, every bead intact.

I like to think of Brenda as the under-garment specialist, but, boy, when she gets through with you, all your proportions are right, and if she whispered in my ear once, she said it a thousand times, "Stand up straight, and hold in your tummy!" As stinging as that sounds, it's better than showing off a potbelly on national television. Believe me!

The casting process is, at best, a tedious and difficult one. Some actors walk in and you know immediately that they are all wrong for the role, but you have to give them the courtesy of a meeting, with your full attention, and you never know, sometimes they turn you around. And for whatever reason, actors may get so nervous that they experience uncontrollable body twitches. I'll tell ya, Peter and I would go home sick from just witnessing the pain and agony some people put them-selves through, all in the name of being an actor. There were kids who auditioned with obviously bleached hair, fully made-up, dressed in clothes to make them appear younger, or the ones who were so sugary in personality you thought, Another five minutes with this kid and I'm gonna get a cavity.

When Madeline Zima came in to meet us for the role of

Grace, she was very distraught that we'd written a joke about her "close and personal friend," Rebecca DeMornay. "You know, I costarred with her in *The Hand That Rocks the Cradle*," she said. "I'm sorry, but I can't say this joke; it goes against everything I believe in." We sat there with our mouths open. This kid's hysterical.

Oh, and one day while filming a scene on *The Nanny* I looked out of the corner of my eye, and there sat a girl who looked exactly like Daryl Hannah.

I said to Madeline, "Doesn't she look just like Daryl Hannah?"

"Fran, it *is* Daryl Hannah," Madeline said. "She dropped in to see my work. We're doing a film together."

Boy, this kid's got connections. Luckily, Madeline hadn't seen *All About Eve*, because when she wasn't looking, I gave Daryl a big, toothy smile. Ya know, in case Madeline was too girlish for the role.

When Charlie (Charles Shaughnessy) auditioned, he arrived wearing yellow rain boots. Here we were, looking for Cary

Me and the Sheffield men in New York City. Look, he's wearing those yellow rain boots.

N.Y. looping the cartoon 5/95

Grant, and this guy arrives dressed like Elmer Fudd. The boots were so dorky that we actually wrote them into the show once, just so Fran Fine could say, "You're always so *GQ*, when did you become the Gorton's fisherman?" I suspect he may never live down those god-awful yellow boots as long as I'm around. But there was no denying the chemistry we had with each other. It wasn't until he said (in response to my complaining about my weight) that American women are too obsessed with being thin and "If you ask me, could all stand to gain a few pounds" that we immediately booked him for the part!

Charlie and Daniel (with his trusty duster) rehearsing.

When we were auditioning for Niles the butler, we saw every Tom, Dick, and Harry. Tall, short, young, old, Haitian, Indian, fat, and skinny. We didn't care about the type but were all just waiting for someone to come in and own the part. Take the words and make them his own, like they were written for only him to say. When Daniel Davis came in, there was a sharpness and specificity to his performance that could not be ignored. He was younger than we had imagined the character, but he did make it his, he owned it all right, and got himself the part of Niles. It was several shows into the season before he let any of us know that he wasn't really English at all but actually from Arkansas. Who knew that this Laurence Olivier–sounding

With Daniel Davis and Dad, recording "The Nanny" cartoon Christmas special, "Oy to the World."

man could, on the turn of a dime, sound exactly like Gomer Pyle?

The search for the Brighton part became one of the more challenging. We hated everyone we saw. Either they were good but too old, or young enough but too sweet or wimpy. It was a nightmare. Who was going to play Brighton? Then one day, Mark Hirschfeld, the casting director, called about a kid who had been flown in from Minnesota by the network to test for another series but had already been rejected for that part.

This is when he was still a little twerp.

"Okay, let's meet him, what have we got to lose?" we answered, and an audition was scheduled. That kid was Benjamin Salisbury. As he entered the room I said, "Hi, *Benji*," and he pointed his forefinger at me and said, "Don't take me there."

"Oh. Okay, *Ben* it is." I looked at Peter and thought, This kid's a cutie. After his reading we all nearly wept! That's how perfect he was for the part. Ben was adorable to look at, charming in person, and strong and confident as the irrepressible Brighton. To think he and his mom were almost on a plane back home, but now they weren't going anywhere. Rob was so thrilled, he offered them his beachfront condo for the weekend until a deal could be put in place. I have no doubt that someday Ben will be running a studio. I just hope he gives me a job.

Now, the role of Maggie was an inspiration of Jeff Sagansky's and not part of our original family. We agreed, though, that a young, shy teenager would be a funny contrast to a brazen and flashy Fran. We developed the character for a young Grace Kelly just on the verge of becoming a woman. We saw redheads, brunettes, and Jewish Grace Kellys, made-up, manicured, and coiffed Grace Kellys, when (just as we were about to think that after they made Grace Kelly, they broke the mold) Nicholle Tom walked in. There she sat, naturally beautiful, awkward, and shy (sweaty palms and all). We'd finally found her.

Nicholle Tom experienced her first real kiss as Maggie on the show. We cast this really cute guy. When she got a look at him, the girl could not stop giggling. The director, Lee Shallat, took great pains to make them feel comfortable about the kiss. When she called action, the two of them went at it, tongues and all.

"Cut," the director said, but they were so into it, they didn't hear a thing. I elbowed the director.

"Well, I guess we cast the right guy!" We finally had to physically tear them apart.

Sylvia with Lauren Lane. Nothing makes my mother happier than big hair.

The real C. C. Babcock, Lauren Lane, at our wrap party. Me as Mary Hart.

Nicholle, smeared with lipstick, said, "I didn't hear you yell cut."

"I bet you didn't," I said, and we all had a good laugh.

I never thought we would ever have the good fortune of finding a C. C. Babcock as greatly performed as Lauren Lane did it. She had it all: beauty, edge, comic timing—she was even a blonde! An absolutely perfect ice princess and foil for Fran. More people ask me if C.C. is the same bitch in person as she is on the show than almost any other question, and I always explain that in spite of the fact that she plays a woman you love to hate, in person she is quite the opposite of her character. Lauren is somewhat Bohemian, shy, and unassuming. She exercises ardently to maintain her great figure and takes all the insults and potshots we write for her character quite on the chin. We're both doing dairy-free, our sisters had babies a month apart, and our menstrual cycles tend to revolve around each other's, so all in all, I would say we're really quite compatible.

As for the secondary characters, I always wanted my dear friend Rachel Chagall to play my best friend, Val. Val is my "Ethel

"She was working in a bridal shop in Flushing, Queens..." My best friend, Val, is played by one of my best friends in the world, Rachel Chagall.

Mertz," and I always thought Rachel was just naturally quirky enough to give the character a particularly interesting dimension. Rob and Pru were for the idea but wanted to hear her read the part before being officially booked.

In the pilot I think Val had all of three lines, which I must say Rachel performed beautifully, but I interjected (just to shed some reality on the situation), "If anyone has any doubts about Rachel's abilities, they can rent the movie *Gaby,* in which she played the title role and earned herself a Golden Globe nomination."

She was booked right there, on the spot. And Rob (the big baby) wanted to be the one who got to tell her, and did.

Me and the real Yetta in Miami. The hair is getting bigger by the minute.

Ann Guilbert, who made her first appearance as Yetta in the second episode, has since become a more permanent fixture, loved by everyone. The first time she was on the show, *my* grandmother (the real Yetta) was quite insulted.

"Why'd ya have to put her in a home? I don't live in a home, I got my own apartment!" she said as she flipped her Bic and took a long drag off her cigarette.

It didn't matter to her that the character would get bigger laughs if we made her a little forgetful. Nothing mattered until that day she desperately needed a last-minute appointment at the beauty parlor (on a Saturday, yet) and got in on account of she's *Yetta,* "the Nanny's" grandma! As her personal fame and glory rose in the neighborhood with each appearance by Ann Guilbert on the show, so did Yetta's appreciation for her coun-

The real Sylvia with the fake Yetta, Ann Guilbert.

terpart. Recently, my seventy-eight-year-old grandmother discovered the joy of a cold beer in front of the TV. I told her that if it makes her feel so good, she should buy a six-pack, to which she responded, "I already did, and there's four left!" That week we put Yetta's beer in a script for Ann.

Ann is a character unto herself, too. Those bottle-thick glasses she wears on the show are actually hers that she wore after some eye surgery many years ago. She said she saved them in the hope of someday doing a character who might wear thick glasses. Well, that time was now. The only problem is, Ann cannot see a thing through 'em, and during rehearsal might be found acting to a lamp.

Last but not least, we needed to cast the role of my mother, Sylvia. Peter and I always wanted Renée Taylor to play Sylvia. Not only is she a brilliant comedienne, but her voice tone has a similar nasal drone to mine and my mother's. I remember how nervous Peter was about my mother's reaction the first time she saw Renée do Sylvia. He feared that she would be insulted by the "look" we gave the character. Mind you, this look was based on my mother's own style, but not everyone sees themselves as others do.

There was Renée, all dolled up in a loud, printed, brightly colored float (muumuu, to anyone not from Queens), huge hair resembling a blond tidal wave, heavy makeup, jewelry, and slippers, and there was my mother, a mirror image of Renée, digesting it all, when she suddenly and with great relief turned to Peter and said, "I'm so glad you didn't exaggerate my hair!"

Once on a stroll through Central Park with my parents we were admiring an adorable little beagle when my mom said, "I prefer a high-haired dog."

Sylvia and Sylvia.

Peter turned to her with mock astonishment, and said, "What a surprise."

My mother laughed till she wet her pants, the barometer by which to judge a good joke in our family.

Renée is another one of those people who is funny without really trying. One time during a rehearsal she actually fell asleep in the middle of a scene. I nudged her and said, "Renée, you were sleeping."

Renée replied, "Can ya believe how relaxed I am?"

I just love her, that's all.

Me and Ma number two. Hair that defies gravity. We call it the tidal wave.

Well, everything was falling into place, but it became clear to Peter and me that *The Nanny* was fast becoming an all-consuming experience, and if we ever wanted to see our friends again, we'd better employ them. So Steve Posner, our mentor and the head of the theater department at our old high school, became the dialogue coach for the Sheffield kids; Howie, a Dartmouth summa cum laude, was a phone page until he got promoted to executive assistant to Peter and me; Rachel's husband, Greg, a former attorney, worked as a production assistant until getting promoted into the DGA stage-managing training program; Zack Norman, the guy who played my husband in *Cadillac Man*, plays Uncle Jack; Dorothy Lyman, of *All My Children* and *Mama's Family*, is the third-season resident director of *The Nanny*, replacing Lee Shallat, a dear and tal-

Steve Posner, our favorite acting teacher in high school, continues to be the favorite acting teacher for the kids on the show.

ented director for both *Princesses* and most of the first two seasons of *The Nanny*.

I'll tell ya, when tape night for the pilot came, people asked
if I had many people I knew in the audience, to which I always
responded happily, "Everyone I know is working on the stage!"

And that's the way I like it! We were now ready to shoot the
pilot (I just hope I'm not ovulating) . . .

Dress rehearsal for
the pilot. Notice that the stairs are
in a different place.

Chapter 19

The Pilot

The night of "The Nanny" pilot.
It was magic.

It was pouring rain the night we shot *The Nanny* pilot. Thunder and lightning rattled the soundstage, but inside we were all aglow. I sat in my dressing room applying my makeup. I do it myself. This way, I have some quiet time. An event was about to take place. Flowers and fruit baskets filled my dressing room. This was the night Peter and I had been waiting for. The big bang. We thought we had a great show, but, then again, we were a little prejudiced, I mean, writing, producing, and starring in it and all. You never know what you've got with comedy until you put it in front of an audience. There was a knock on my door. The assistant director yelled, "Five minutes, Ms. Drescher." "Ms. Drescher," don't you love it?

EVERYONE was there. Friends, family, network and studio execs, all together like one big party. We were about to start taping the show. You could hear a pin drop.

Then the stage manager counted down, "Five, four, three, two . . ."

I took a deep breath and thought, Carpe diem again, honey.

I entered the Sheffield mansion à la Fran Fine, the earthy "blue collar" girl who mixes for the first time with her "blue blood" counterparts, all done up in a short skirt, high heels, and big hair (which have since become synonymous with the character). I said my first line, and hilarity ensued. Oh, thank

People said, "Who covers their furniture in plastic?" Obviously, they've never been to Queens.

God. It was working! Okay, half the audience was friends and family, but the other half was bused in from a prison. They didn't *have* to laugh, no one was holding a gun to their heads . . . although . . . You could feel the audience was with us, we had to hold for every joke. The audience laughter was uproarious. Boy, when it all comes together right, there's nothing like it.

No one could believe how well we were received. I mean, it's one thing when an audience is there to see a popular show like *Roseanne* or *Mad About You*. Then, they're already familiar with the characters and the relationships and used to seeing the show each week in their living rooms. But *The Nanny* was an unknown quantity, and yet they got it and enjoyed it like a familiar old friend. When the cast took their curtain call after the show, we all felt we had a winner. But there were many other pilots out there being taped, and the people taping them thought they were winners, too. It was now up to the gods.

Then came the long wait while CBS got all their fifty pilots in. They were only going to choose six. Peter rubbed and paced, and I watched Peter rub and pace. Then, after about six agonizing weeks, the phone rang. It was CBS. They wanted Rob, Pru, and Peter to come down to the network. What about me? What, are they replacing me with Nell Carter?

Well, I went to a museum with Howie while they all went to their meeting. (Who can concentrate on art when your whole future is at stake? I should've just gone to eat something. The ultimate distraction.) Meanwhile, the network was asking all kinds of questions about *The Nanny*.

"Where do you see the characters going?"

"Wherever the hell you want 'em to go."

"We want to change the opening titles."

"So do we."

"We'd like some big changes on the set."

Rob, Pru, and Peter looked at each other. *"We hate the set. Whatever you want."*

Then Jeff stood up. "Would you guys mind waiting out in the lobby?" he asked. "I'd like to talk to Jon Feltheimer alone."

They all left like bad children who had given the wrong answers. The three of them sat there for what seemed like hours, but was, in reality, only five minutes. Jon walked out with a very serious face. *Oh, no, it's over.*

Peter said, "Don't tell me," then Jon broke a smile.

"You're picked up and on the fall schedule. Not to mention that *The Nanny* was the highest-tested CBS pilot in three years." The three of them practically did an Irish jig.

Somehow Peter found me at the museum. I screamed to Howie so loud, making somewhat of a spectacle of myself, "*It was picked up. We did it. I'm dropping dead!*" echoed through the room with the Chagalls and Monets. Oh, what a moment! I just wanted to linger in it forever.

Peter and I sent baskets from Manhattan Fruitier to everyone involved in picking up the show, and Elaine proclaimed that we would dance in the streets and talk to no one—which I never quite understood but assumed one couldn't do until one had "arrived." We just couldn't believe this was actually happening to *us*. After a decade and a half of riding the merry-go-round, we had finally grabbed the brass ring. I felt like an Olympian runner who had jumped every hurdle and made it

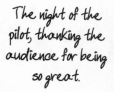

The night of the pilot, thanking the audience for being so great.

to the finish line first! Should we crack open that bottle of Dom Perignon some rich dinner guest once brought that we were saving for a special occasion? Or do we go to a fancy restaurant, buy something for ourselves, pay off the Visa bill, have sex? Yes, yes, yes, yes, and YES!

Chapter 20

Setting Up Shop

We pulled up to the studio gate in our 1978 Buick. I lowered my window to tell the Nazi, I mean, guard, "Hi, I'm Fran Drescher."

"Who?"

"Fran Drescher."

"How do you spell that?" he asked.

"D-R-E . . . Fran Drescher of *The Nanny*?"

"Never heard of it."

"It's a new show. Oh, never mind." Thank God, they eventually let us drive in. Peter and I looked at each other kiddingly. Really, doesn't he know who we think we are?

"There it is, honey," I shouted, pointing to space #463. "They put your name up—P. Jacobson—you've got your very own studio parking space!" No longer did we have to park

Peter in his studio parking spot.

miles away and take a tram to the studio. As we walked to our office, we enthusiastically waved hello to every passerby. People must have thought we were nuts. But we weren't nuts, simply on cloud nine.

Studio personnel were eating breakfast outside at the commissary cafe, little go-carts crisscrossed their way from one soundstage to another. There seemed to be patches of flowering gardens everywhere. Peter yelled, "There goes a star!" Where? Where? And then I saw him; coming out of the commissary was Paul Reiser of *Mad About You*. It was so thrilling you would have thought we'd spotted Elvis himself. I waved. He had no idea who I was. Billy Crystal was also on the lot shooting *City Slickers II*, but we only saw the outside of his trailer (which was the size of my entire house).

When we arrived at our office, it had odd pieces of furniture thrown together with no real thought or style. "I wanna redecorate!" I said, but Peter was quick to try and pacify me. "It's fine, it's no big deal!" I said, as I was already schmoozing on the phone with Tom of Studio Furniture.

Next thing ya know, we're at the furniture warehouse pointing out the pieces we wanted. That was so much fun, I'll never forget it. A gorgeous French desk was sitting among big

Rob and Pru in my trailer. Feed them and they will come.

oak monstrosities. "That's gorgeous, I'll take that," I said. Before long, Peter had that swap meet/garage sale look in his eyes and started pulling lamps, wing chairs, a couch, a coffee table, and the sweetest country French whitewashed armoire, a leftover from *The Young and the Restless*! Two hours later, Peter and I were placing some flowers we picked from the lot into a vase on the coffee table, and our new office was complete. It looked like a model home. And it was ours. Our very own model office. Out came the camera. I posed Peter behind his new desk: "Pick up the phone, make like ya making a call," while I reclined on the couch reading, simulating the producer laboring over a script. Pathetic, huh?

Next stop, my star trailer. I've always wanted a star trailer, but I guess ya have to become a star first to get one. I remember Danny Aykroyd during the *Doctor Detroit* shoot generously offering myself and the other girls in the movie his trailer while shooting on the Universal lot, since he also had a big office as well, and what a treat it was. As I opened the door to my trailer with my key, it became clear to me that this wasn't exactly like the star trailer Danny had loaned us years before, or that Billy

Crystal was using just around the corner, but, then again, I'm not Dan Aykroyd *or* Billy Crystal.

It was really cute, though, in a Ma and Pa Kettle kinda way, and apparently the same as the trailer that Paul Reiser and Helen Hunt have. Everybody gets the exact same model, so there are no complaints or jealousies. Ugh, they treat us like such children. Meanwhile, I think Paul's is nine and a half inches wider than mine. But who's measuring?

That first week of rehearsals was mind-blowing. Everything coming together just like a real television show. I brought my famous chopped liver in for the cast and crew, thinking that this would help us to feel like a family. Yeah, *my* family, indigestion and all!

Ménage à trois.

Chapter 21

Duplicity with Publicity

I'll never forget my first photo shoot. Cari Ross, my publicist, arranged for me to have gorgeous pictures for my press kit. I thought that over the years some beautiful photos had been taken of me, and why not just use one of them? There was a long pause on the other end of the phone, and then Cari said, "Fran, trust me, those pictures are all wrong, they're not high fashion enough, the hair is out of style, and you did your own makeup for God's sake!" But do you like them? . . . In ten minutes a shoot was arranged.

Peter and I arrived at the photographer's studio schlepping assorted garments from my wardrobe as well as *my* makeup, *my* jewelry, and *my* shoes. So I was a little distrustful of the process, but can you blame me? I was used to doing everything myself, and now I was suddenly expected to abandon all that Jewish-neurotic-control-freak persona and act normal?

"Darling, you are so beautiful," said a short man with an Italian accent. This was Enzo, a hairdresser I would use again and again throughout the years.

"I like big hair," I said, as if parking myself in Anthony's beauty parlor on Avenue U in Brooklyn. Enzo, dear, sweet Enzo, looked at me with a wry and quizzical smile.

"What you mean by BIG HAIR?"

Uh-oh, I thought to myself, we're not in Kansas anymore.

"Well, my hair is somewhat fine, although there's a lot of it"—Enzo is trying to track what I'm saying but stares blankly at me like I'm from another planet—"so if ya tease it, ya know, really pack it in"—at that moment, I kid you not, his jaw literally dropped, and suddenly, in two seconds, I had turned into a character from Bob Altman's *Nashville*—"ah . . . ya know what? Do what you want."

Enzo was quick to take hold of the reins. "I make lots of soft curls you're gonna love, darling, trust me. Then perhaps later, I sculpt an upsweep we shoot from the side."

"Fine, fine," I mumbled to myself. I'm getting *soft*, which I equate with *flat*, and a "do" that only looks good from the side! Where's Claudia Schiffer's hairdresser when ya need him? Apparently, my efforts to help the guy out by painstakingly blow-drying my hair that morning with the diffuser so it would come out extra curly were in vain, too, because Enzo immediately started to wet it down, at which point the stylist (the person who brings the "right" clothes to wear in the shoot) began to pull things off her rack and show them to me through the mirror for my approval.

"I thought this would have a sexy but clean look, with the collar spread and the cuffs left loose and unbuttoned . . . what do you think?" Was this woman for real? This is who charges five hundred dollars a session for her expert fashion sense?

"Isn't that just a man's plain white shirt?"

She answered me with two simple words, as if they would explain everything: "Calvin Klein."

Meanwhile, Peter is feverishly pawing through the rack of clothes in desperate search of anything tight, a couple of sequins, or a lousy rhinestone, God forbid.

"Ya know, I brought some great outfits, too. Maybe we should go through them . . . Ow!" I suddenly yelped.

"Sorree," Enzo said coyly.

"That's okay." I didn't need that ear. This was fast becoming a Greek tragedy, and I turned my attention back to the stylist from hell. "Can you pull my gold lamé pantsuit for me?" I said with strained composure. "It's a Donna Karan," I added with confidence, knowing that that was a good label to drop.

She held it out and examined it with authoritative expertise and said, "Wasn't this from last season's collection?"

Last season's sale rack, I thought to myself, and then meekly lied and said, "I guess so . . . uh . . . put it back in my bag."

Suddenly Peter shouted, "Wait, here's something," and proceeded to pull from the stylist's rack a burgundy evening gown.

"Oh, that's great," she chimed in, happy to find some enthusiasm from somewhere. Great? It's a tent!

"That's not really my style, isn't it a bit voluminous?" I said to Peter, widening my eyes as if to say "Have you lost your mind?" But Peter was now grabbing the reins and suggested to the stylist that she'd have to pin all the extra material in the back, creating something fitted that fanned out just below the knee.

"All right," I conceded, "that could work," and jumped on the bandwagon. "Let me show you some earrings I brought that might work," I suggested.

"EARRINGS???" the stylist gasped.

I thought to myself, Who said earrings? I didn't say earrings . . . if only life came with a rewind button.

"No one's wearing earrings anymore," she said condescendingly.

Who knew? Have the jewelers been told? Gee, all those years of reading *Vogue* and *Elle* never prepared me for any of this. I felt like the biggest shlub. Look out, here comes the cow from Queens!

As I stepped out of Enzo's chair adorned with curlers, I crossed to sit in the makeup chair. Now, I was instructed to arrive with a clean face, no makeup, essentially a blank canvas for the makeup artist. Well, how will *she* know how *I* like it to look, or rather how the makeup looks best on *me?* So of course I brought photos, and of course it was in vain. Carol Shaw and I were at opposite ends of the lipstick color palate and neither was budging. The negotiations were delicate, but we managed to go from Pale Beige and Fire Engine Red (guess whose was whose) and compromise on a nice Naughty Nectar.

Suddenly Jeffrey Thurnher, the photographer, appeared out of his studio to check out the beauty team's work. The guy looked around nine. Young, thin, and trendy, but warm and likable. Clearly, the photographer is the head honcho among the hierarchy of fashion à la mode dictators. He breezed through each department. First Enzo said, "Jeffrey—I want to make very soft, natural, not even with a brush, just use my fingers to separate the curls."

"No brush?" I mumbled to myself. It's not gonna be big enough . . . Jeffrey responds with enthusiasm.

All right, so I was a little off with the hair, I thought as he moved over to Carol. He studied my face for a moment, resting his chin on his hand, then spoke. "I like the eyes, simple, clean." I guess the false eyelashes are a pass. "The face is young and fresh. But . . . I think the lips are too dark." All right, so I know nothing! As Carol tissued off my mouth with forceful vindication, I watched out of the corner of my eye as Jeff approached the stylist. I saw Jeff's head nodding over the

Test shots for "McCall's."

dress, but heard him requesting
in addition to that something
really casual, loose and plain.
"Maybe just a man's shirt,
opened and unstructured."
What is this, a conspiracy? I
wondered. Then the bitch
makes *me* out to be the bad
one who killed that idea in
the first place.

"Look, I don't mind
wearing a white shirt," I
said in my own defense. "But can I at
least wear my white Dolce and Gabbana?" (At least that's
got a ruffle!) They reluctantly agreed. By the way, if you ever
wonder why we never look like the models in the magazines,
well, the entire hair, clothes, and makeup procedure took, I kid
you not, six hours.

I think everyone was pleasantly surprised to see this
uptight, opinionated chick from Queens transformed into the
confident, fluid, photogenic subject I became in front of the
camera, and somehow it all clicked. Oh, it was so glamorous, I
felt like the spokesmodel on *Star Search*. Enzo looped a curl
around my eye like a monocle for some shots, and Jeffrey kept
telling me, for some reason, to reach into my jacket and hold
my tit in some other shots. But by this point I knew better
than to question any of it, and lo and behold, the shoot was
indeed a success, and the photos are used to this day.

Now, of course, I'm much hipper to this whole crazy high-fashion scene and have collected a group of favorites in every department that Cari calls upon for various shoots. I've even had my own lipstick color named after me: Fran, by Lorac, Carol's cosmetics company. Isn't that cool? I still schlep shoes, jewelry, and bras, though. It's like my dad always says, "It's better to *have* and *not need* than to *need* and *not have!*"

Test shots for a Hanes commercial.

The end justified the means.

Chapter 22

Help, I Need Somebody

So, all things now being what they were, life was sweet. However, not two days into the rehearsal week, I realized I had no time anymore to maintain my personal life. I mean, I had been semiretired for the better part of my adult life, working in spurts, a month here, two weeks there, and unemployment in between. Now, with *The Nanny* in full swing, suddenly there wasn't time to go to the dry cleaner's or the market or get cash from the teller machine or take a good crap, for that matter! I, who always had a wonderfully organized home life, was beside myself.

Then I heard through the grapevine that both Paul Reiser *and* Helen Hunt were provided with a personal assistant by the

Rehearsal, we all sit around a table and read the script. Those are the cameras with the big Baggies around them.

studio. Hello! Apparently, most stars are unable to contend with the routines of daily life and require a "right arm" to go and do for them. Someone whom they can trust to organize the most intimate details of their lives, who is available whenever and wherever they may be needed, and who, above all, does it dirt cheap, all this for the privilege of being on the inside, learning, growing, and eventually (if they luck out with the right boss) getting promoted to a higher level within the company.

That day I was on the phone with my agent, Bob Gersh, pleading my case, and the next day my Robbie was born! After meeting with two or three guys (I knew I wanted a male assistant so I would feel safe being driven to my door late at night, and I wouldn't feel guilty having him schlepping heavy bundles), Robbie Schwartz was clearly the perfect candidate. He was twenty-two at the time, a tall, thin kid, pretty ordinary-seeming, but I was very intrigued by his wry wit, the diversity

Everyone always thinks that Robbie's my brother and Elaine's our mother.

of his intelligence, and the fact that after having graduated from college he chose to live for a year in the eternal city of lights (and love), Paris. How Bohemian of him.

Meanwhile, so much for that. "Did ya walk the dog, buy my Tampax, and gift wrap that birthday present you picked up for me yesterday?" Poor guy, what a job, and it wasn't long before I felt him starting to resent his position. What was I to do? I needed him to think on his feet, sharpen his follow-up skills, show more enthusiasm and pride in his work. I'd already put the painstaking time into teaching him the details of my life. Where we bank, dry-clean, shop, who our business contacts are, doctors, etc. I couldn't go through that again, and besides, there was something soulful in my connection to him. I just had to make it work. Then it hit me. Robbie was a guy who'd grown up in New Jersey and Malibu, playing tennis and learning to ski. Plus he had lived on his own in Paris for a year, and was a Jewish prince, to boot! Oy, this one will never acclimate himself to picking up Chester's dog shit.

Lying in bed with Peter one night I told him that I needed to give Robbie a raise. "A raise?" Peter yelped. "How can you give him a raise when he's driving you crazy?" Well, I began to explain my theory, first to Peter, then to Robbie himself.

"Look, I have certain needs that you must satisfy [God knows what he thought I was leading up to], but I realize that some of those responsibilities may make you feel like you're working beneath your station, and, therefore, in exchange for doing an excellent job each week, I will supplement the meager salary the studio pays you with cash so you'll at least know I appreciate you in the most practical way possible." A couple of hundred dollars a week later, the station beneath which he worked started lookin' mighty fine.

Howie, Mom, and Robbie at a
backyard barbecue.

Chapter 23

What's My Schedule?

I worked harder in the first two seasons of *The Nanny* than all my other years of work combined. Oh, please God, just let my face hold up! It seemed every waking hour of the day was accounted for with one responsibility or another, not to mention the enormous amount of press and the talk shows I was getting, which became a second job in itself. Poor Robbie had to keep tabs on my constantly changing schedule, which was so packed with appointments that I relinquished all responsibility to him.

"What's next?" was always my question. A typical day's agenda would be carefully noted in Robbie's book, down to the last fraction of the hour (the guy was on top of everything, including my menstrual cycles!).

"After you finish editing notes on last week's show, you have rehearsal, I have a whole list of autograph requests I think you should start on during your first five-minute break, lunch is at one o'clock, you're doing a phone interview with Tom Shales of the *Washington Post*, he's also the head of the Television Critics Association [God bless Robbie, he always made sure I knew the things I needed to know, even a current sports or news event headline that might come up during a talk show]. While you're talking to Tom you have to set your hair and start your makeup, then at two o'clock it's back to rehearsal for a four o'clock run-through [each Wednesday the network, the studio, and the writers-producers come to see a run-through of the week's play. It's rough, and many of us are still holding the script, but it's the only way to determine if the script is working and if all parts are funny enough], at four-thirty you finish hair and makeup and change into your gown. At five o'clock, Danny [my favorite limo driver] will pick us up for a five-thirty arrival at *The Arsenio Hall Show*, after which the car will bring us back to the studio so you can be a part of the rewrite tonight." And then he would close the book non-chalantly, like he had just said that I had to pick up a chicken at the market or something!

"That's all?" I answered facetiously, and methodically began my day. I remembered all the years of semiretirement (the only thing filling my date book was my periods) when a celebrity on a talk show would say they hadn't had a rest in three years and I wondered how that could be, but now I know.

It's so hard to get to this point in your career that once you arrive you have to (as the surfer dudes say) hang ten and ride the wave! Well, that's what I was doing all right. Sometimes things got so hectic I would very often be booked for magazine photo shoots on the weekends because the weekdays were just too filled. And even though I continued to be busier than ever, we actually produced a spin-off of *The Nanny*. But we couldn't even bask in the afterglow of how far we'd gotten as producers because the very next day I was scheduled to do a photo shoot for the *cover* of *TV Guide*! Little ol' me from Flushing, Queens. In two short years I had become the queen of Queens, or as *Elle* so flatteringly described me on its cover, "Fran Drescher, TV's Sexiest Funny Lady." Believe you me, the next day that cover was at the House O' Frames getting framed.

And very often we had to go to New York to do certain publicity like *David Letterman, Regis & Kathie Lee,* and *Howard Stern*. Now, a lot of people are afraid of Howard, but he and I have always had a cool thing going, and after having made an appearance, I usually get an enormous amount of positive feedback from his listeners.

I've always seen through his alter-ego radio persona and am endeared by the real him, a devoted family man living on Long Island whose kids never miss *The Nanny*. Once on his show he accused me of being one of those pretty girls who in high school would never have looked twice at a guy like him.

"Actually, you're wrong," I responded. "I've always been attracted to the nebbishy type, myself." And when he autographed my copy of his book, he wrote, "Love from your little nebbish, Howard Stern."

Sometimes we would wrap a taping of a *Nanny* episode by nine or nine-thirty, jump in a limo with Robbie, and take the red-eye to New York for a whirlwind of three hectic days, flying back to Los Angeles first thing Tuesday morning where we would be met by another limo that would drop us off back at the studio to begin rehearsals on the new week's play!

By this point, Robbie was traveling with us everywhere, helping to organize the details of each trip. As I finish my interview on *CBS This Morning* and jump into a limo, engine running, ready to roll, and get whisked off to Howard Stern's show, Robbie connects me on the cellular to the *Letterman* people for my pre-interview (when we discuss the stories I want to talk about in advance so David can formulate his

Test shots for "Elle."

Test shots for the cover of "Elle."

Peter and Rob, when we were shooting in NYC. Look at the crowd.

questions and pre-
pare some jokes of his own) during
the fifteen-minute drive over to the radio station.
Meanwhile, Peter is feeding me jokes of my own for Howard,
Robbie is enlightening me as to last night's Knicks game tri-
umph (a topic that might come up on Howard's show), and I
wonder, If this is what it's like for me, what must it have been
like to be one of the Beatles?

There was actually one occasion when I was arriving at JFK
Airport at around four-thirty in the afternoon and had to be
at Rockefeller Center by six to tape the *Today Tonight Show,* a
special edition of NBC's morning show. Now, anybody who's
ever tried to get from JFK into Manhattan knows the kind of
traffic you can hit during rush hour on the Grand Central
Parkway, and apparently so did NBC, because in an effort to
ensure my timely arrival, a chartered helicopter was arranged,
and exactly eight minutes later we were landing at some heli-
port in the city. Man, was that ever exciting! A little nauseat-

ing, but exciting. Just like in the movies, the chopper touched down, its propeller continued to turn, wind everywhere. We climbed out, ducking our heads as we dashed into a limo waiting on the runway. I'm not quite sure it was necessary to duck my head, but that's the way they always seem to do it in the movies, and I wanted to experience the full flavor of the bean!

By the time I finished taping the show and got to my hotel, there was already a message from Cari that someone from *Letterman* had seen me at NBC and, since I was in town, asked if I would fill in the next night for a guest who'd dropped out at the last minute. I said sure. I love doing *Letterman*, especially since he moved over to CBS. The show has an excitement to it that remains unparalleled by any other of its kind. It's got a fresh, alive feeling to it that probably only comes when the host is being paid 14 million dollars (I kid you not).

I just can't pass up a bargain.

Once during an interview with Dave, I was telling him about the dinner party for the network executives where I accidentally set myself on fire, when Dave interjects that he could think of nothing worse than sucking up to the CBS executives over dinner and that he would never do that.

"Honey, if I had your deal, I wouldn't either," I responded, and the audience went nuts, laughing and applauding. They love it when you can stick it back to him, and I usually can, which is why they keep asking me back.

David and I do the dance well. One time I came on with my croutons (did I mention that Peter and I have a gourmet crouton company?), which he readily opened and began to taste, then suddenly pulled a fast one on me and pretended to be pulling a hair out of his mouth. Now, nothing gets a live audience going quite like gross humor, and they loved this one big time. Brain, don't fail me now, I thought, as I heard myself saying, "If you've got a hair in your mouth, what were you doing in your dressing room before the show? . . . Don't blame my croutons!" The audience ate it up. What a comeback, we were dancin' pretty now.

Everything about doing *Letterman* is like an event, from the moment his limo picks you up at your hotel until stopping in front of the side entrance of the Ed Sullivan Theater. Now, here's where you really get to feel like

I created a crouton business, Loaf & Kisses. The day I showed my mother that she was on the label with my great-grandmother, she broke down in tears.

a Beatle, because there are always scores of fans (your fans), who heard Dave announce your guest spot the night before, piled behind police barriers, wanting you to autograph photos they've got of *you*. So you try to sign as many as you can before security pulls you and your entourage into the building.

Inside, Dave likes to keep the theater very cold, I mean, I'm talkin' *Ice Station Zebra* time, so I'm usually freezing the entire time until I finally sit my ass in the hot seat. In my dressing room, a modest three-by-five closet with a TV monitor, bathroom, and vanity, crowd Peter, Robbie, Elaine, Cari, and I. I arrive wearing something really cute and short to greet my fans on the outside but upon arrival change into something long, sexy, and very revealing for the show. The Todd Oldham (usually I'll wear a Todd Oldham gown, a favorite designer of mine and a truly great guy as well) I chose to wear was a slinky snakeskin print that fit like a second skin. All Todd's collections are great because their silhouettes are classic in shape, but his fabrics are really young and fun. Perfect for me.

Someone comes in to have me sign my contract. Everyone gets paid scale, I think it's like six hundred dollars, but as Elaine always says, "It's better than a kick in the ass!" By this time Robbie has returned from the greenroom (a lounge set up next to the stage) with a plate of nibbles for all us hungry Jews. Peter zeroes in on the shrimp, and in two seconds, they're gone. We all look at Robbie like he fucked up royally.

"How can you only bring two shrimp? Are you insane?" Nothing gets us more irritable than being denied our shrimp.

So he half-heartedly asked, "Do you want me to go down the four flights and get us some more?"

And much to his shock (although I don't know why), we all responded in unison, "YES!!!"

In his absence we rationalize among ourselves that this was why we brought him and what he's getting paid for, when there's a knock on the door. As Cari goes to open it, Elaine is muttering, "I hope he remembers the cocktail sauce," but it's

Elaine, Peter, and Cari enjoying ...

not Robbie, it's Daniel, the guy I did my pre-interview with, who begins to review the questions Dave will ask, and which story of mine answers each one. This format, which is the same on all of these types of interview shows, is known as a loosely scripted show. It's a springboard for possible spontaneity and a safety net as well. In the event nothing much develops, we know we have the script to resort to.

I'm usually touching up my makeup while he runs everything down, including places Dave might go jokewise. He then leaves, passing Robbie entering with an embarrassing amount of shrimp.

"Robbie," I say coyly, "what could we possibly do with all those shrimp?" Poor Robbie ... Then the sound technician enters, ready to body-mike me (a small clip-on microphone that they attach to your clothes and that's connected to a small transmitter about the size of an audiocassette). In vain the poor guy searches for a place to hide the transmitter, but the dress is too tight, and finally I suggest just holding the damn thing.

The shoot for the cover of this book.

In the background, Elaine, Cari, Robbie, and Peter are attacking the shrimp like they were just released from Auschwitz when the TV monitor starts to air Dave's opening monologue, at which point Daniel pops his head in again and says, "You ready?"

"It's time?" I ask, thinking, Isn't there a commercial break first? because it's so freezing in that backstage area I can never differentiate whether my chattering teeth are from nerves or frostbite, but I leave without a fight and am offered luck by all.

"Give 'em hell, honey, knock 'em dead, break a leg," garbles Elaine as she removes a shrimp tail from between her teeth.

Next I find myself standing in front of a long mirror next to the curtain in a semi-frozen state, checking my hair, my lipstick, my dress, when Dave introduces me. The curtain is drawn from the back side by a nice man who tries to look encouraging right before you're getting thrown to the wolves, and I enter.

Arms up in my famed entrance stance, I seek out my camera with peripheral vision while greeting the audience, who seem warm and receptive. I kiss Dave, who meets me halfway and helps me step up onto his platform. Oh, please Lord, don't let me trip. There's a cup of water marked Guest #2 that awaits me. Antonio Banderas was Guest #1, so I decide to use his instead. I wave hello to the band (Paul and I worked together in *Spinal Tap*), comment on the great audience, and Dave and I begin to do our thing.

During the commercial break, Dave usually leans in to say something, and people always ask, "What's he saying?" Well, one time he asked how that husband of mine was doing, to which I responded, "Great, but what's your story? Are you married, single, living an alternate lifestyle?" I've always been a natural-born matchmaker.

He laughed. "Oh no, not for me. If I ever got married, I'd just have to get divorced again."

The stage manager begins counting us in, "Five, four, three, two . . ." and points to Dave. We were back on and never spoke of it again.

Three minutes later the second half of my segment is over, and ten people immediately rush to Dave to prepare him for the next guest, and I wave good-bye to the audience, have my microphone removed, and am ushered off the stage by Daniel, who leads me through the dark hallways, up the elevator shaft, and into the security of my little entourage. Now I can take a deep sigh of relief. I jumped the biggest hurdle again and didn't fall flat on my face. Immediately afterward, we gorged ourselves at Chanterelle in TriBeCa. Except for Elaine, who was popping a Mylanta gel cap. One too many shrimp.

People ask what we do on weekends when we're not working. One word: sleep! Usually, we are so exhausted. We sleep so well after a show that we'll roll out of bed and book a massage, my favorite indulgence. Then roll back into bed, have sex, and go back to sleep until Monday morning. Oh, there's nothing more underrated than a good bed.

Chapter 24

Bad Things Happen
to Good People

Sometimes, being a celebrity does have its drawbacks. For some reason, it seems to give license to those who can profit from your exploitation by unearthing some of the darker, more painful traumas you might have encountered along the way. Just when you've worked desperately to pick up the pieces of your life and put the past behind you . . .

Me, Peter, and Robbie sat in the greenroom of the *Howard Stern* show. Gary, the producer, popped his head in to see if I needed anything and to say I'd be going on in a few minutes. This was not the first time I'd been a guest on *Howard Stern*, but it was the first time my radio interview would also be televised on his E! channel show.

The thing about doing an interview with Howard is that if

you're a no-bullshit open book, as I am, you gain his respect, but if you come across as masked, phony, and fake, he's going to try and tear you down, he's going to go for your jugular. We listen in the greenroom to Howard and Robin discuss today's newspaper headlines as Stuttering John walks by and waves hello. Now, when you do *Stern* there is no pre-interview, so there's no telling where the conversation might go, and you really have to be on your toes. It's good to read the paper yourself before showing up because he could ask your opinion on any number of issues, and you don't want to come across like an idiot. Especially since you're out there flying solo while he's got two writers opposite him scribbling jokes and answers for him to say while on the air live. But this was the first time I was doing the radio show when it would be simultaneously taped for television, and there lies the rub!

Suddenly we hear Howard telling Robin that they've got Fran Drescher about to come out, and he was going to talk about this horrible thing that happened to her—

"She was raped," Robin chimed in. "I hope she'll talk to us about this horrible, tragic rape."

"I think her husband was held with a gun to his head and had to witness all this."

"Oh, my God," Robin gasped.

"Well, we're going to talk with Fran all about it right after these messages." Howard switched off to some prerecorded commercials as Peter's and my hearts sank.

Robbie asked, "Do ya want me to try and reach Cari?"

"Where the fuck is she? She should be here." Peter was getting very angry, then he made an abrupt decision. "Let's go, let's just leave, I can't believe Howard's doing this, and it was ten years ago." But the hotter Peter gets, the more levelheaded I become.

"I gotta go out there, if I don't he's just gonna rag on me for the rest of the show, and I'd rather just face the music." The subject had come up before in print, but never on anything of this scale, and yet I had nothing to apologize for or be embarrassed about, I was the victim, for God's sake, and maybe in some way I might touch some other victim by exemplifying my own survival.

It was January 5, 1985, a day that will live in infamy. For some reason, I can't remember why, my girlfriend Judi stopped by in the morning on her way to work. I had the last few shots of film in my camera and used them on the three of us so I could take the roll in for processing. Judi was our first friend when we moved to L.A. and to this day remains one of our oldest and dearest friends.

Judi, who was single and looking for love in all the wrong places, confirmed dinner back at the house at the end of the day, not knowing the apocalypse that would later occur. Peter and I set out on the course of our day: dry cleaner's, Fotomat, bank, auditions.

In those days, Peter was still an actor, but he was always tormented by all the rejection that comes with being one, yet addicted to it as well. After leaving his final meeting, he turned to me and said, "This has been the worst day of my life." That profound statement would haunt him for a long time to come, as he blamed himself for bringing on the event that would truly define the worst day in our lives. Of course, that's what Marilyn the shrink calls "magical thinking." Bad things happen to good people, and whatever was said that afternoon had absolutely no connection to what happened that night.

At the end of the day we made a brief stop at Danny and Donna's to see some furnishings that had been delivered to their newly purchased home in the Hollywood Hills. They asked us to stay for dinner, but we declined the offer, since it was Judi we had committed to see. *If* only we had stayed. *If* only we had canceled on Judi. The saddest words I've heard or seen are "Oh, but *if* it could have been." Oh, well, hindsight is always twenty-twenty.

We had just finished dinner, I'd made a meat loaf, and by

around eight o'clock we were still sitting around the kitchen table when Chester, who was only two at the time, began barking at the front door. So I got on the intercom and asked, "Who is it?" but there was no answer. Twice this happened, and twice I chalked the disturbance off to a neighbor.

But they were out there, diligently working at unhinging our door. Why didn't I look out the window, or the peephole, or the upstairs terrace? More questions that can never be answered. You can't rewrite history, you can only learn from it or be doomed to repeat it. I can tell you this much, we now heed Chester's warnings with the attention and speed of a fail-safe operation. Suddenly there was a loud bang. Peter later said he thought it was an earthquake, but from my seat at the kitchen table I could see what was happening.

The front door was broken down, and two men with guns were running toward us. I let out a scream that was more like a primal roar, when every nuance of your being is focused on one thing. The hardest thing for Peter to get beyond in therapy was that image of me (the only one who knew what was happening), the look on my face of sheer and absolute horror in that initial moment. But we were taught to walk our minds past that point all the way to the part when *they* left and *we* lived.

Now, it was just that week that I happened to be watching a morning talk show and felt the impact of what a police detective was saying about most victims not making good witnesses. I found it so interesting that the greatest difficulty in finding a perpetrator is mostly due to the fact that the victim becomes crippled by such fear during the attack that they are rarely ever able to give a clear description. The detective went on to say how important it was to get a good look at your assailant, notice any distinguishing features or scars or birthmarks. Memorize his face so the police will have a better opportunity of apprehending the guy. Because of that TV program I did just that, and managed to work out a police sketch that was such a dead ringer you'd think the creep sat and posed for his own portrait! He had small, oddly wide-set eyes and teeth that were slightly bucked so as to keep his lips apart even when his mouth was closed. Medium-black skin, short curly hair, Italian loafers, slacks, and a Windbreaker.

The police later informed us that there had been many violent attacks in our area, and that they had been granted a three-night stakeout budget by the city. If the assailant hadn't shown up in those three days it's likely that they might never have caught him. Every corner had a plainclothesman with a police radio, just watching and waiting, each with a copy of my police sketch.

When a white car with Compton plates pulled out of a driveway, the vehicle began to be tagged as it headed toward the freeway. Just before it reached the freeway ramp, it was pulled over, and it was all over. Out of the car climbed my rapist, a convicted felon on parole, with jewelry hanging out of his pocket and his fly still unzipped. Tragically, some poor woman had to become his last victim before he was apprehended. The detective who arrested him said that he kept saying he didn't do anything, that they had the wrong man, but the police sketch, when held next to him, looked like a dead ringer. The detective said, "This is you, you motherfucker, and you're under arrest!" God bless the Van Nuys P.D.

Two busloads of witnesses (victims) testified in court, and this sorry excuse for a man was put away without parole for 120 years. His partner and brother got 15. The police said they said they were on a rampage. . . . Two weeks after the attack, Peter and I made love for the first time. He must have noticed my face, eyes closed, contorted with inner agony, and instinctively he knew that in my head, I was back at the scene of the crime. He said, "Open your eyes, it's only me . . . FRAN! Open your eyes, it's me, it's only me." I opened my eyes and kept them open, easing back into life.

Even though I'm usually the strong one, emotionally, in

our relationship, when I simply can't be, and Peter therefore must, he is positively heroic. We will never again be the same, but thanks to the generosity of our friends Danny and Donna, who opened their hearts and their home to us for almost three months, Peter and I began to feel safe and protected, slowly creeping out of the nest a little more with each passing day.

I remember sitting in the Aykroyd den with what little was left of my worldly possessions safely tucked in my handbag, which I kept by my side at all times. To this day I must admit to having a phobic attachment to my purse and continue to carry it from room to room even in my own home. In retrospect I realize that I was in a state of shock, I was a nervous wreck, and my perspective on things was completely distorted. All I wanted to do was leave, run away, anywhere seemed better than here.

In my darkest moments, when I felt sure we would all be assassinated, I didn't think about the movies I never made or the fame I'd never know. None of that entered my mind, so why should I stick around this war zone any longer—I thought I should pack up my bags and move to Massachusetts, open a boutique or something. It seemed that any lowlife could get himself an illegal gun and attack those of us who are hard-working, upstanding citizens but who are, in reality, sitting ducks.

I described my feelings to a circle of girlfriends who surrounded me with love and support. "I feel like we're all sitting around a campfire and you are all encouraging me to put my hand in the fire, but only I seem to know what pain I'll endure if I do . . . I just can't go through something like that again, I don't want to fear so deeply, I won't withstand this depth of pain again!"

Elaine, God bless her, made me promise to trust her and give it six months. I didn't want to, every bone in my body told me that she and all my other friends were crazy, but I did trust her, and I realized that it was possible, due to such an experience, that I was overreacting. Under such circumstances, it's best to trust your loved ones' instincts over your own, no matter how wrong it feels. And I did. So Elaine talked us out of making any rash, life-altering decisions until some of the dust had settled and we could see life more clearly. And she was right, of course, and for that we are most grateful.

Also, by some amazing coincidence, another TV show affected our recovery. About two weeks before the break-in, I happened to be watching a local L.A. morning show, which was interviewing a psychologist on ways to avoid the Christmastime blues. They had audience phone-ins, and the way this woman so clearly articulated her answers and how much sense each response made impressed me to the point of actually writing her name in my phone book. I remember thinking to myself, If we ever need a shrink, this is the one to call. Two weeks later, I was making an emergency call to her, and she has, to this day, continued to be a significant and positive influence in our lives and in our marriage.

The other place we called was Victims' Compensation, a wonderful program offered by the state of California to help pay the medical and legal expenses of victims of violent crimes. If they approved the application, our therapy bills, for a time, would be paid for by the state.

At the interview the woman conducting it began asking me questions. "What do you do?" she asked, face in her notepad.

"I'm an actor, I, um, uh . . . "

She looked up at me and said, "Does that happen often?"

"What?"

"You didn't finish your sentence, you can't seem to finish your thought."

"Oh . . . I don't . . . know . . . uh . . . what?" I muttered. Believe it or not, *you,* the person this is all happening to, are unaware of your own change in attitude and personality.

Needless to say, we all got the victims' compensation. So we all began getting therapy. I would look at myself in the mirror and imagine seeing my image shattered into a million tiny, splintered fragments, for that was what I felt like. Would I ever get back to the me I used to know? Yes, but not for a long, long time, and some scars just never go away. Peter diligently went and received psychological help for many facets of his life. He was an open wound, so a lot came up, starting from early childhood. I, on the other hand, was still quite cemented in my superwoman mode and, once I felt a little more solid, attended sessions only sporadically. It would be years before I would explore my own vulnerabilities. But eventually I came around, too. I'm not a superwoman, I'm merely a woman. It is my nature to give, but now I appreciate my entitlement to take as well.

And through our love and therapy, we managed to turn a negative into a positive. I now am far more compassionate of other people's pain than I ever was before. Each experience and choice in life I now make is influenced by the insight that life should never be wasted, for it is a precious gift that might end at any given moment, and in times of strife one must choose to run toward one's mate, no matter how painful, rather than running apart, the result being a deeper, more bonding union.

The intimate details of this horrific experience have never been told, it's really nobody's business, but so many people have written about it that I wanted to include elements in the hope that it might help someone. I do, however, grandstand my opinions. About parole—I don't believe in it. You do the crime, you do the time. Also, rehab belongs with white-collar crime, drug users, misdemeanors, and first offenders. The rest should do hard labor and throw away the key. I believe in educating women to the tragic truth that one out of every three will be raped in their lifetime, a pitiful reality as we approach the twenty-first century.

More people responded to my interview on *Howard Stern* than all my other interviews combined, and always with a great deal of protection, love, and compassion. So to all those sisters who have suffered the indignity of a sterile emergency-room rape test, I applaud your bravery and implore you to march on victoriously, a survivor as a woman in a sometimes violent man's world. Ya know, once you bottom out, there's nowhere to go but up. Remember, there is a light at the end of the tunnel.

God bless Dan. It was our first season, and he made an appearance as a refrigerator repairman.

Chapter 25

The Changing of the Guard

By the end of our first season, we heard that Jeff Sagansky was leaving CBS. With all the timing of a winning thoroughbred, I might add. Since he was our most ardent supporter over there, the news really freaked us out until Jeff took over as the head of Sony Pictures (our parent company), and we thought, This could be a good thing . . . but I wasn't sure if Peter Tortorici, his successor, shared Jeff's enthusiasm.

Peter and our son the
night of the Romeo and
Juliet taping.

My mother got to hug Ponch!

Peter playing Romeo to my Juliet.

Steve, Eydie, and Franny, the new singing sensation.

So in an effort to help ensure a second season, I decided to throw a dinner party for some network and studio executives before the network left for New York, at which point they determine what shows will be renewed and what shows will be canceled. My thinking has always been that when trying to ingratiate myself with anyone, feeding them is the first rule of thumb. I built the entire evening around Tortorici's availability, because a night like this, without the president-to-be, would be a complete act of futility (not to mention a waste of money). Well, I managed to pin him down to a date, and everything else fell into place. All the kings came. There was Sagansky, Tortorici, and Feltheimer, but the biggest coup of all was the president of Columbia Broadcasting Systems, big daddy to them all, Howard Stringer, who I had called in New York and invited to join us in the event that he happened to be in L.A. the night of the party (if there's one thing I got, it's chutzpah!).

I figured it was only proper protocol (I mean, I wouldn't have wanted to ruffle any feathers . . .), since Howard and I had always shared a genuine fondness for each other (dating all the way back to *Princesses*) and it was my pleasure to welcome him into my home. Howard is an impressive man, with a large, imposing stature and Brooks Brothers Oxford tailoring. He is the greatest testament to the advice for success, "Look British and think Yiddish," since Howard is both and a king among kings!

Now, I wanted everything to be perfect at this party. All my choices had to be right. Since our home is small and our backyard is like a Monet garden, filled with comfortable overstuffed wicker, large canopies of fragrant flowering trees, a big old-fashioned back porch, and an Italian terra-cotta fountain, there was never any other consideration but to have the party outside.

I catered the affair from Patina, one of the best restaurants in L.A., with a very successful catering division as well. The place charges a bloody fortune, but you get what you pay for, and with an average price of a hundred bucks a head, I expected perfection, and got it. My mother's response was, "For a hundred bucks they should kiss your ass in Macy's window."

The first thing Tortorici said to me that night was during cocktails and hors d'oeuvres (he had just shoved a shrimp cannelloni into his mouth). "Fran, this food is spectacular, where's it from?" (Something in the way he asked implied surprise that we weren't eating franks and beans.)

I proudly replied, "Patina," to which he responded, "Oh, well, of course." That made the tab a mere incidental as I watched him go for a gravlax and caviar blini.

There were around fifty guests and approximately ten kitchen staff: a party coordinator who supervises the timing from one course to another and oversees the entire event, a chef and his assistants, waiters, bartenders, you name it. I couldn't believe what an organized piece of machinery this catering thing could be, and I, who was always revered by others for my great home cooking (coupled with the fact that I couldn't afford to cater the opening of an envelope), enjoyed for the first time in my life being a hostess in my own house whose sole responsibility was to be charming to my guests and let everyone else do all the work! Dear God, please let the show get picked up, because I can get very used to this.

We rounded out the guest list with some interesting and successful people who had nothing to gain by schmoozing with a CBS executive, thereby making the night seem less like just another boring business gig. It was a good group of people, and the place looked smashing. I had small, white votive candles lit everywhere, and exquisite Italian arias as background music. Howard arrived still on crutches and in a cast after an unfortunate slip on the ice in Lillehammer, where I guess he was attending the events, since CBS had the lock on

Elaine and Allan.

the Winter Olympics. As he hobbled in with Dave Poltrack, an unexpected guest and a pleasure to see (Dave is the exec who analyzes all the ratings numbers for the other execs), whose presence was yet another feather in my cap, and someone Rob Sternin zeroed right in on as only a good executive producer would, the entire energy of the party heightened with excitement. I mean, Howard gets invited to guest on *Larry King Live* to discuss world communications and dines with our nation's president, so you can imagine the buzz when he took a seat in *my* backyard!

It was a couple of hours into the evening, the night-blooming jasmine perfumed the air with its sweet and sensuous aroma, each food course was more memorable than the last, and everyone was really mellow and satiated from this gastronomic orgy. Howard seemed to be basking in the music of the arias on the CD player (I didn't know opera was his favorite), his vodka, and the peacefulness of our magical and lovely garden when I decided that now was a good time to sit with him and schmooze while enjoying my cheese course (this was before I went dairy-free).

"Howie, you seem so relaxed," I kvelled as I sidled up to him. Now, Peter Tortorici once told me that "only three people ever had the nerve to call Howard Stringer 'Howie' and they're all overseas. But believe me when I tell you, they didn't start out there," which I took more like a joke than a warning and used at a CBS press conference once when I was introducing "Howie" to the podium, to which I got a huge laugh. I know he knew it was a term of endearment and not one of disrespect, as I have always sung his praises with only the greatest adoration.

Anyway, just as I placed my cheese plate on a nearby table, the fuzz from my sweater brushed against one of the votive candles and instantly all the fuzz went up in flames. It was as if a bonfire had been started in the center of the garden as guests

We were in Italy when my agent faxed us that "The Nanny" was picked up for a second season.

from all sides turned to see this frightening sight. My Peter and many guests were up on the porch taking selections from the dessert table as time seemed to break down into those surreal fractions of seconds, and in that moment horror crept into everyone's hearts. I remember Elaine saying in her own New York monotone (with the casualness of "Pass me the pickles"), "Fran, you're on fire." With that, Howard stood up on his good leg and I bent forward, and together we pulled the sweater off my body. Fortunately, the sweater was made of heavy wool, so my skin never burned, and in pulling it off, it smothered the flames.

Now of all days not to wear a bra . . . there I stood before Howard Stringer, Peter Tortorici, and Jon Feltheimer, as well as the remaining guests and catering staff, totally and completely nude from the waist up. Peter Tortorici said, "I thought I would get to know you better, but I never thought I would get to know you this well."

The party continued into the wee hours with the kind of unified exhilaration that comes when a group encounters the extraordinary, the next day Liz Smith printed an exclusive in her column about how Howard Stringer had saved my life, and everyone was buzzing about the party, each exec making himself the hero as the event got told. P.S., we got picked up for a second season! But what the hell am I gonna do next season?!

And that was when Peter Tortorici very cleverly moved us into CBS's 8:00 P.M. Monday-night time slot, replacing *Evening Shade*. It was that move that exposed *The Nanny* to a much larger audience than we were ever able to receive on Wednesdays, and it was at that point that we moved into the "big pond." Suddenly, Monday at 8:00 P.M. became the most competitive time slot on prime-time TV, because the other networks thought that the CBS lineup was getting tired, and an aggressive effort was made to bust it up.

When the new fall season began, my Peter and Rob Sternin were nervous, unsure if the move was right for us. Maybe it was better to be a big fish in a little pond than possibly the other way around. Suddenly we were up against *Coach*, *Melrose Place*, *Fresh Prince*, and *Star Trek*, and that was just on network TV; there's also local programming and cable. But Pru and I never faltered. I knew how great *The Nanny* was and I believed it deserved to compete with the best, and may the best show win!

Well, the week came when all the shows premiered. I will never forget *Variety*'s headline: "Nanny Spanks Coach!" and the *Hollywood Reporter*, which wrote "The Nanny *CRUSHES* its competition!" Today, thanks to our viewers, *The Nanny* has become a favorite TV show all over the world.

Mom and Dad on their honeymoon.

Chapter 26

Sylvia and Morty

My parents, Hansel and Gretel,
in our Monet garden.

I call my parents Hansel and Gretel because they're the dearest, sweetest little couple. Likewise, in *The Nanny*, Fran Fine's parents are also named Sylvia and Morty. Morty to this day has never been seen on the show because he's always in another room watching sports on TV. The real Morty, however, has

Dad's acting debut.

217

Morty Drescher

Since when do extras get their own directors' chairs?

DAD   MOM

The week he played Uncle Stanley we had a birthday party on the set.

It was a very special cake from Cake Art here in Los Angeles.

DAILY VARIETY

75 CENTS
FRIDAY
OCTOBER 28, 1994

A CAHNERS PUBLICATION · LOS ANGELES, CALIFORNIA · NEWSPAPER SECOND CLASS P.O. ENTRY

THE NANNY MAKES IT TO THE TOP 20

MORTY DRESCHER STEALS SHOW ON HIS 65TH BIRTHDAY.

CHESTER DRESCHER SIGNS HUGE SPIN-OFF DEAL!!!

TRI STAR MAKES RECORD NANNY SYNDICATION DEAL STERNIN AND FRASER BUY MONTECITO.

PETER MARK JACOBS AT 37, COINED CBS'S NEW GOLDEN BOY.

NANNY SPANKS COACH AGAIN.

DRESCHER ENTERS 10TH SEASON. STILL FORCES EMPLOYEES TO EAT HER CROUTONS.

NANNY CAST SWEEPS EMMYS!

made two appearances on *The Nanny*, once in a nonspeaking role with my mom, sitting in the waiting room of Gracie's therapist (Mom, who is not quite the natural my dad is, kept watching me during the scene and kvelling. I would catch her out of the corner of my eye, chest puffed—smiling from ear to ear. I said, "Ma, what are ya looking at me for? Read a magazine. You're supposed to be a patient." Then Ma said, "It just gives me such pleasure. I can't believe *you* came out of me"), and the second time was when we established him as Fran's Uncle Stanley (my dad's brother, plaid sports coat and all). Uncle Stanley suggests to Brighton that he consider getting into Styrofoam. Brighton says that it's not biodegradable. "Who's asking you to eat it?" responds my dad, and gets a huge laugh. That part was shot the week of his sixty-fifth birthday, God bless him. Dad took to the whole thing like a fish to water, and I can see now that I got my personality (and voice) from my mom and my natural acting ability from Dad.

Sylvia and Yetta.

After the show, we all went out for dinner, at which point my mom commented that she thought our family in the party scene was portrayed as too crude. Peter explained that for the sake of the comedy it was important to punctuate the contrast between the blue-collar and the blue-blood characters.

"Well, ya made us navy blue collar!" my mom said, and

My mom, Yetta, and Aunt Denise. Now you know where I get the big hair from.

then proceeded to stick her entire fist into her mouth in an attempt to pick something from between her teeth. Totally unaware, my mom has the best comic timing of anyone I know.

The greatest pleasure I derive from my success is the joy it brings to my parents. Between *The Nanny* becoming a hit and my sister having a baby, my folks are ten feet off the ground at all times. As retirees down in Florida (they wanted to be different), they have become satellite celebrities unto themselves, just by association.

One time they were at the cashier's in their local Penney's signing the credit card receipt when the clerk saw the name Drescher and said casually, "You spell your name like my favorite actress in the world, Fran Drescher!" My parents in that moment realized just how famous I'd become.

My dad explained with loud Drescher enthusiasm, "We're the parents!" and faster than the speed of light, my mother whipped out the pictures (not from her wallet, mind you, the woman carries a stack of fifty four-by-fives in an envelope held together with a rubber band). They're so cute, my parents, wherever they go they take their own census, casually asking some unsuspecting cashier or the odd yenta out by the pool,

The Drescher uncles.

"Have you seen that show, *The Nanny*?" If the answer is "Yes, I love it," that's my dad's cue to identify themselves as the "real" Sylvia and Morty, which of course cues my mother again to whip out the pictures.

They are wacky, my parents, and truly the major source of

The Drescher aunts.

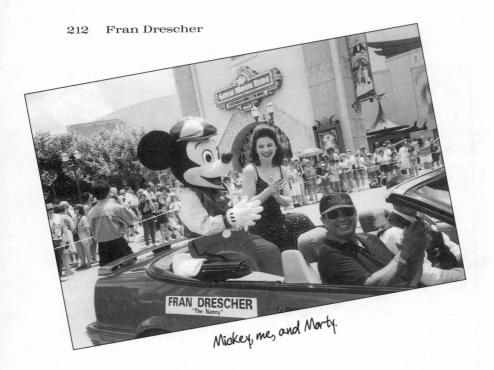

FRAN DRESCHER
"The Nanny"

Mickey, me, and Marty.

so much of the material we write on *The Nanny,* as well as the stories I tell on talk shows. Jay Leno loves to hear a good Sylvia story, particularly when he's trying to get off embarrassing subjects. Like the time I told the *Tonight Show* audience that Jay gave me the best stage kiss I'd ever had, and that included Dan Aykroyd and Robin Williams! Needless to say, the audience went nuts, but that's the truth, as are all my stories. Jay got embarrassed and followed with the "How are your folks doin'?" question, which was my cue to tell the Disney World story . . .

"I just saw them down in Orlando, when I was invited to be the celebrity of the week at Disney World. I drove down a motorcade with Mickey and said, 'Here, hold my glasses,' but ya know, he only nodded on account of he's not allowed to speak!"

"He couldn't have gotten a word in edgewise, anyway," Jay quickly replied, getting a good laugh. Jay always enjoys ribbing me that I talk a lot, and we have a good time playing off it. I, of course, laughed along with the audience, then moved back into my story (this is what I call dancing the dance).

"And for that, they gave both me and my parents our own vacation villas, which were so pretty, except for one thing—all the bric-a-brac was glued down to the furniture. I'm thinkin', What, are they afraid you're gonna take something home? as my mother tried to pry off an adorable ashtray that would've looked gorgeous in their Florida room. It was kinda like being in a *Twilight Zone* episode . . . We got our very own Mouse-keteer VIP guide, who bore a strange resemblance to Snow White and took us through tunnels that run under the entire park.

"I saw the rooms where they keep all the characters' costumes. I wanted to put on Minnie's head, but the bitch wouldn't let me [pause for laughs], and it's so unreal seeing all these bizarrely costumed employees dressed up for their appropriate ride or other activity, moving like creatures from *Dawn of the Dead* through these smelly, dingy tunnels. No wonder the kids who work there call it Mouseschwitz! [Pause again.] We got on all the rides without standing on lines and were comped at all the restaurants. My mother said, 'This was the best vacation we ever had! Everything was free, plus you were famous!'" The audience gave a huge laugh and applauded as Jay cut away for a commercial.

And Mom wasn't kidding, either. My parents are people who seek out the biggest discounts, especially when purchasing airline tickets. Peter and I marvel at their consistency. Not once, not twice, but on three different occasions, my mom and dad booked tickets on some obscure Florida airline that managed to go bankrupt before my parents' return flight. Peter quips, "You'd think the name 'Shnorra Airlines' would tip them off!"

Recently, they opted to fly on an airline that had some unfortunate luck with losing some planes in crashes. Their thought was that now the airline'd be extra careful and probably give bigger portions than the other airlines.

One time, they stayed at a Ramada Inn (probably because my dad had stock in the company and wanted to support his investment); anyway, they were so impressed with the generous hospitality bar they insisted my uncle Aaron clean it out and take it home with him, since my folks don't drink much anyway. What a wonderful stay it was . . . until checkout time when the bill included several hundred dollars for the minibar! How these people could live so long and remain so sheltered is beyond me, but they honestly thought a hospitality bar meant that it was compliments of the hotel to show how hospitable they were.

The real Yetta with Uncle Aaron. We joked about him on the show: "You can't eat forty-two latkes and sit that close to the menorah . . ."

Meanwhile, my dad wrote the Ramada people explaining their point of view, opening the letter with "Maybe we're naive, but . . ." "*Maybe* you're naive?" I exclaimed. "Are you telling me you've never stayed in a hotel with a minibar before?"

At which point my mother calmly responded, "No, they only give a coffeemaker at the Circle 7 Motel." Oy. P.S., my dad's loophole in this whole mishegas was that they never got a minibar price list along with the minibar, and Ramada graciously refunded their money. There's a reason I call them Hansel and Gretel, but meanwhile, the story will someday end up on *The Nanny,* and so it goes . . .

Chapter 27

Streisand, the Princess, and Me

The most fun thing about being a star is the perks you receive. While Peter and I were still struggling, we used to watch Danny Aykroyd get lavished with gifts and complimentary things all the time. We'd look at him and look at each other and say, "Nu? The rich get richer." F. Scott Fitzgerald was right. Simple things continue to excite and thrill us no end. For example, getting a reservation at a hard-to-book restaurant is always a rush. We've had complimentary bottles of wine sent over, free desserts, extra courses just sent over by the chef or owner.

In the old days there were certain "in" places we wouldn't dare go unless we were in the company of Danny and Donna, but now, when our executive assistant Howie drops my name while making a reservation, they roll out the red carpet. It's a

Us with Dan and Donna. Dan rented
a yacht for the opening of
"Ghostbusters." It's nice to have rich
friends. Natural poses, eh?

The opening of "Ghostbusters."

fun ride. I think of myself as the "flavor of the month," but for as long as it lasts, I enjoy being a star. Once, on a trip to New York, Peter and I decided we would try to get tickets for Barbra Streisand's show at Madison Square Garden, tickets that were most difficult to get, when we were told by a Sony executive that she records under the Sony label and that Sony Signatures was handling all the merchandising as well. Before we could say evergreen, two ground floor–level comped tickets were messengered to our hotel. This really takes the cake, we're going to hear Streisand sing, live! Somebody pinch me. We're not worthy, we're not worthy, we thought as we melded into the thousands of paying customers at the Garden's entrance. What an exciting night, the thrill, the rush, the fans . . . are beginning to notice

me. Soon, everywhere we turned large groups were looking, pointing, and moving toward ME. It never occurred to me, but Peter said, "We're in New York at a Streisand concert. I guess a lot of her fans are your fans, too. Who knew?" And let's not forget, it *was* Gay Pride Week.

Yetta and me posing for "TV Guide." Now she's a celebrity and gets appointments at the beauty parlor on Saturday with no advance notice.

I went to the bathroom before the show, and a bunch of women armed with concert programs and pens were anxiously crowded outside my stall. Unsuspecting, I flushed the toilet, pulled up my jeans, and innocently opened the door. "Can I have your autograph?" "Oh, I love you, I never miss your show." "Meeting you beats seeing Streisand."

I looked at that one and said, "Oh, come on."

"No, it's true," she insisted. "Wait till I tell my kids, sign this, sign this," she says as she shoves the program in my hands.

"You want me to autograph the twenty-dollar Barbra Streisand program?" I responded as if asked to perform an act of heresy, but that's what she wanted, and so I accommodated her request, as well as the other ladies, all atwitter that I had to pee at the same time they did.

As I exited from the rest room and began to fill Peter in on the amazing thing that had just happened in my stall, and while I was ordering one of the most delicious hot, salty, potato knishes from the snack bar that I had had in years, a group of fans began to gather around me. Peter said we better go sit down. Sipping my beverage and nibbling my knish, we walked down several levels of the arena, advancing toward the exclusive ground-level seating. Well, I guess more and more people were spotting me, as a tidal wave of fans began shouting and waving, "Fran!" "Fran!" "Up here, we love you!" For a moment, I thought Francis Ford Coppola was in the audience. Peter said, "No, honey, they're talking to you." It was very flattering.

We showed our tickets to the usher, who guarded those hard-to-get ground-level seats on the top-of-the-line carpet Barbra had had specially installed. Peter and I took our seats toward the back of the section. However, there must have been five hundred people in this section alone, and that was enough to create a bit of a mob scene around our row. I couldn't believe all these people shouting from the stands and those in our section wanting my autograph on Barbra's face! Well, I guess someone took notice from the event because a guy from special services came over and asked, "Are you Fran Drescher?" I said yes, at which point he proceeded to say, "Would you like to sit closer?"

Without skipping a beat, Peter and I were up and moving, following this guy like our lives depended on it. "Sit here," he said, pointing to two seats on the aisle in the third row. I kid you not!

"No one is sitting here?" I asked.

"Don't worry about it," he answered in typical New York style, "they didn't show."

"But what if they come late and the usher asks me to move? This could look bad and get in the tabloids," I questioned.

But the guy assured us he'd take care of everything, and in a flash shoved two ticket stubs for these new seats in our hands. Will wonders never cease? Boy, where there's a will, there's a way. We thanked him profusely and offered him a tip, which he wouldn't accept, then suddenly, just as the lights were going down, two ladies with the same ticket stubs arrived. I knew it, I knew this would happen, I thought, and began to gather my things, ready to sneak back to our old seats. This same guy then actually showed up with two more seats, extending our aisle by two and putting the two ladies in them! Only in New York.

The orchestra was amazing, with Marvin Hamlisch conducting, the sound was incredible, and then she entered. God's gift to all little Jewish girls in need of a leader. The voice of the century, Barbra Streisand! As she entered at the top of a long white staircase and began to sing, the audience went nuts with adulation. I grabbed Peter's hand and squeezed it—this was going to be a night to remember. She only sang her best songs, kibbitzed with the audience, and showed on a large screen highlights from her movies *The Way We Were, Yentl,* and *The Prince of Tides* while she sang the scores live. Oy, I'll tell ya, by intermission I was exhausted from all the applauding, whistling, hooting, and hyperventilating I was doing. We just stayed in our seats at the break when our friend the miracle worker returned with VIP backstage passes for after the show. Peter and I looked at each other and both thought the same thing, God bless *The Nanny!* (And we do, every day.) When the concert was over, she got what must have been a ten-minute standing ovation. Well deserved, I might add. As soon as the audience lights came up, Peter and I dashed into tunnel number one, where we had been instructed to go for the backstage reception. Will we actually get to meet her, oh, I wish my mother could have come to experience this, I thought. But this moment belongs to us. Us and Babs, that is.

We held up our VIP backstage passes with Barbra's picture on them (which I still hang on my work bag and my refrigerator) to various security guards as we continued moving through the gray industrial-looking backstage of the Garden. Suddenly we arrived at a square room created by white curtains, which was filled with a few dozen people who all seemed unsure as to what to expect. On one side was a table filled with flutes of champagne, which I grabbed, then advanced to the other side of the room to a table filled with trays of enormous cold shrimp and petite roast beef sandwiches. I hesitated about the shrimp at first, I mean, I didn't want to smell like fish when I met Babs . . . Eh, I'll wash it down with champagne and suck on a Certs.

Within minutes a special-events guy approached us just as I was shoving a third shrimp in, and said we were in the wrong room.

"But we were given these passes," I tried to explain, already getting indigestion.

"You wanna meet Miss Streisand, don't you?"

Do birds fly? I thought, and he proceeded to escort us into the "A" backstage room where everyone who was anyone was that evening. As we entered a very large room also defined within this cavernous warehouse by beautiful draped white curtains (by the way, every detail of this event was designed by Barbra herself), I saw antique furniture casually arranged in conversational corners and fine paintings displayed on easels as decoration. White-gloved servers carrying silver trays passed drinks and hors d'oeuvres to the New York elite. Gee, had I known all this was gonna happen I wouldn't have worn jeans. Then we spotted her at the far end of the room talking to Geraldine Ferraro. "Let's go," I said to Peter, and began a diagonal advance toward Streisand.

En route, Marvin Hamlisch stepped in front of me to tell me

how much a fan of my show he was. Yeah, yeah, I thought, meanwhile, where's Babs . . .

"Oh, thank you so much, Marvin, great show tonight," I actually tossed over my shoulder, but kept walking with only one objective, to meet Streisand. Oh, my God, I just snubbed Marvin *The Way We Were* Hamlisch (whom I *love*), but continued full speed ahead anyway. (Marvin will appear in a cameo role on a third-season episode of *The Nanny.*) Elaine May was off to one side smoking and chattering away. And Donna Karan, the fashion designer, was sticking close to Barbra. They're like best friends, and Donna designed the gowns Barbra wore in the show.

Geraldine Ferraro was going on and on about something or other to Barbra as I arrived and landed right behind Geraldine. Now, as gigantic a star as Streisand is, in person she's surprisingly petite. She had changed into a pants suit and washed off much of her stage makeup. She looked fabulous. I could not believe I was actually standing this close to a legend, who meanwhile looked like my aunt Marilyn from Bayside. Well, Barbra kind of tuned out Geraldine, looked past her at me, and said three words I shall never forget: "Who are you?"

If I didn't just shit in my pants right then, I never would, and I answered, "I'm 'the Nanny,' Fran Drescher." Then she, the great Streisand, engaged me some more, as Geraldine, realizing she had been dismissed, begged out graciously.

"Didn't I see you on *Letterman* last night?" I'm dropping dead, Babs was lying in bed, probably in her glamorous penthouse hotel suite somewhere high atop the Manhattan skyline, on the night before her concert at Madison Square Garden, watching *me* on the *Late Show with David Letterman*! These are the moments we live for.

"Yes, Barbra, that was *me*," after which I proceeded to describe an episode of *The Nanny* where we paid homage to her, and then I quoted a joke from the show, "So when I tell my mother that I gave my Barbra Streisand concert tickets to Miss Babcock because it was the right thing to do, Sylvia, played by Renée Taylor . . ."

"Renée Taylor?" she interjected with a scream. "I know Renée, I used to open for her, oh, God, don't tell me *I'm* old enough to be your mother?" She seemed to panic, putting me in the awkward position of calming her down the only way I could think of.

Joe and Renée.

"Oh, no, Renée is much older than you," I said with assurance, and continued, "so Renée . . . Sylvia, asks Fran, my character, 'What's the matter? Don't you love Barbra anymore?' And I say, 'Ma, she's our leader.'"

Well, that gave her and the whole room a good chuckle, at which point I offered to send her a video of the show. Which I did, but hadn't heard another thing about it for several months until one day when I received a thank-you note on Barbra Streisand stationery, which read, "Dear Fran, Thank you so much for the very funny and flattering [and "flattering" was added in pencil as if it were an afterthought or she was personalizing her secretary's work] episode. I thoroughly enjoyed. Love, B." So I guess people in the know call her "B." I was hoping to acquire one of the photos taken of us in that moment but, so far, no such luck. I think I'm gonna have to just go ahead and frame the note on its own already.

Well, by this time I sensed that our romance was dwindling down to a last few "I love you, Barbra"s, and excused myself. Upon exiting I managed to share a few words with Donna Karan. I wanted her to know that I had worn one of her dresses to the Elton John AIDS benefit Oscar party, and would you believe she offered her showroom services to me in the future?

That's it, Streisand *and* wholesale Donna Karan. It don't get much better than this, I thought, and I left. Make an entrance, make an exit, and make a wholesale Donna Karan connection. Bada bing, bada boom.

A special-services man led us through the underworld of the Garden and across the very stage where Barbra had performed. I looked out to the audience seats and tried to imagine what it must feel like to stand there, as she did, and face tens of thousands of people all there to see you. It's gotta be a huge rush. The special-services man led us out the side doors away from the maddening crowds and ushered us into one of Barbra Streisand's limousines that apparently just sit and wait for those VIPs who may require an escorted exit.

"He'll take you anywhere ya wanna go—good night and thanks for coming to the concert!" the special-services man said as he closed us in the car and disappeared back into the Garden.

"No one is gonna believe this night happened to us!" we shrieked as the driver sped us off to a trendy bar in SoHo.

That evening was only equaled by the night I got to chat with Princess Diana. It was also in New York City, on the eve of the CFDA (Council of Fashion Designers Association) Awards ceremonies at the New York State Theater in Lincoln Center, benefiting AIDS and breast cancer research. This is a major New York event, and it's an honor to be asked to present an award, so Cari, of course, insisted that I accept the invitation to present Cynthia Rowley with the New Designer of the Year Award. It meant taking the red-eye to New York with Robbie and Elaine after the Friday taping, attending first the Elton John AIDS benefit at the Waldorf-Astoria on Saturday night, the CFDA Awards on Monday night, then returning to rehearsal first thing Tuesday morning. What a whirlwind, and Peter missed it because he needed to work with the writers on Monday and felt that he would be more valuable to them than to me, since I would be traveling with Elaine and Robbie anyway.

Now, the Elton John benefit had a very sophisticated guest

The big CBS affiliates meeting in NYC. Putting on the dog.

list filled with the New York
social elite: Barbara Walters; the former mayor,
David Dinkins; Simon Critchell, the president of Cartier, etc.
Cari and Elaine felt that my choice of evening gowns needed to
be couture and elegant, nothing too oozy with sex or flash, and
Valentino graciously offered me something stunning in black
lace. Elaine came as my escort to both events. We arrived late at
the Waldorf and missed the cocktail hour, as the group was
already advancing to their designated dinner tables. Eh, no big
loss, I can't be charming and keep my lipstick on with a rumaki
in one hand and a spritzer in the other anyway.

We were at the Cartier table as guests of Simon Critchell, an
adorable, elegant Englishman married to a Frenchwoman.
They'd brought their teenaged son along, who sat next to Elaine
and immediately took to her and all her outrageousness. I sat
next to Daniel Boulud, the acclaimed chef of Daniel restaurant

on East 76th Street in New York City. Now, for me to be sitting next to a world-class star chef is as satisfying an experience as any I've ever had. I'm so interested in cooking as well as the restaurant business, and since I had recently taken Jeff Sagansky and his wife, Christie (shortly after Jeff's move over to Sony . . . I'm no fool), to Daniel, we had much to talk about. It was a fabulous gala with some amazing people-watching. At Elton's table (which was right next to ours) sat Sly Stallone, Bruce Willis, and Sting. Bruce had at one time stopped by my table at Orso's to congratulate me on *The Nanny*. Can you imagine such a big star going out of his way like that? If only it had all happened *after* I'd swallowed my mouthful of fried liver and onions.

Elton sang at the piano for about an hour. It was amazing because he was so close in such an intimate room (compared to an arena), plus he sang all his best songs from throughout his career. I love and support the Elton John AIDS Foundation because it's one of the very few charities where an average of ninety-seven cents of every donated dollar goes directly to the people who need help the most, the AIDS patients.

By contrast to that evening, the CFDA evening was a total crush. Because Princess Diana, who at the time was considering a move to New York, accepted the request to be a presenter, the press stood ten deep and half a block long. I'd been to a lot of events in my day, but, boy, when Diana attends it's a veritable paparazzi frenzy. I wore the gold lamé gown from the Cynthia Rowley collection. It was very sexy, with a ten-foot gold voile train (subtle is my middle name).

This is the fashion event of the year, and I wanted to pop. At the hotel, a makeup and hair person named Rob did me. Since I was wearing something really hot-looking, I chose to work against it with a French twist and $250,000 worth of jewels, loaned along with an armed security-guard escort. It's so mind-blowing when you see on TV famous actresses arriving at various major Hollywood-type events wearing exquisite couture clothes and magnificent jewels. Odds are, they're only borrowed, not paid for. Nu? All those years I was struggling and wanting to look decent, I would desperately search the sale racks and overextend my budget. Now that I can afford it, they lend it to me. Go figure!

As I exited from the limo at Lincoln Center, Elaine and security right behind me, I stepped out onto the traditional red carpet, and roped-off fans went insane screaming out my name. I waved and said hello to them all, and thanked them for watching, but continued moving toward the press, who were roped off on either side of the red carpet for about seventy-five feet from the entrance to the theater.

In my life I have never seen so many flashbulbs going off all at once, and TV crews with cameras calling me to them for a quick interview. Now, of course, this turnout of press was due to the princess. However, they all seemed happy to see me, and I worked those cameras for all it was worth. As I raised my arms high up in the air in my now famous and familiar pose, I thought I would lose my balance from all the flashes. "Fran, over here," "Fran, this way," "Fran, right into the lens," the paparazzi would shout, and I wished I could have shared this unbelievable moment of fame with Peter. Two weeks later *InStyle* magazine ran a strip of me from various events, in different gowns, all with my arms stretched toward the sky and the subtitle reading, "No one vogues for the cameras quite like Fran Drescher." Hoo-ha. "You've finally made it!" Peter said.

Now, because I was a presenter, I was invited to a private cocktail party hosted by the princess herself on the mezzanine level. All the top New York designers were there: Calvin Klein, Ralph Lauren, Donna Karan (all of whom head the CFDA), etc., as well as important names on the guest list like Diane Sawyer and Connie Chung. Diane gave me the biggest hello after having met me once at Marilu's book-signing party, and admitted that she tries never to miss *The Nanny* every Monday night. What a doll, I thought. Plus, she has a really funny personality, like it isn't enough to be a gorgeous, intelligent, and fabulously successful shiksa goddess.

Now, while all the hubbubbing was going on at this cocktail party, an obvious person seemed to be absent from the affair, when, lo and behold, who comes walking in, towering over a circle of bodyguards, but Diana herself, the Princess of Wales. Her hair was greased back really simple like that "I'm not even trying" look, meanwhile, sixteen bobby pins were busy diggin' into my scalp as she floated in. Calvin, Donna, and Ralph all

The new news team. Dan Rather, eat your heart out.

waited with backs against the wall to be received. She graciously shook each of their hands and was promptly ushered into a second room, where she took her position in the center, and, like locusts, wall-to-wall people immediately surrounded her.

I leaned over to Elaine, like Lucy to Ethel, and whispered, "I'm cuttin' through this crowd to meet the princess. You either stick close or I'm leavin' ya behind." As I "pardon me"d all the way to the princess, she was just finishing speaking to an unidentified older couple. Around Diana's neck hung a multi-strand pearl choker held together by an enormous blue oval sapphire about the size of a Twinkie surrounded by large round diamonds, each about the size of a watermelon seed.

"Look at that necklace," Elaine whispered. "Do you think it's real?"

I looked at Elaine like she was insane. "E," I said, "ya think I'm wearing real jewels but the princess is wearing paste?"

Just as the couple began to pull away, I wedged myself in

and grabbed her hand to shake it. She had long princess-like fingers and seemed to be quite tan all over. I noticed that she wore very little makeup and what seemed to be no base or foundation (which I, of course, considered to be a mistake). Instantly, a blond Englishwoman amazingly enough introduced me to the princess, coupled with a brief one-liner on who stood before her.

"Oh, this is Fran Drescher, she's the star of a very successful comedy series here in America in which she plays the title role of a nanny who works for a British widower and his three children." Wow, was I impressed, even if the princess wasn't. I wished the show was on in the U.K. because then she'd have had a clue as to who the hell she was meeting. Oh, well, too bad for me, but it was still thrilling. I told her that "when this time, your time, is chronicled in the history books, you shall be written as the heroine."

With that she looked at me as if for the first time, deep into my eyes, and said, "Thank you, that's very kind of you to say." I laughed my trademark laugh, at which point she looked at me again, this time as if to say, "Did that sound just come out of you?"

Quickly I assessed whether I could get out one more thing before being dismissed and ultimately decided to forge ahead. I mean, after all, we had just connected so well that I could schmooze for one more minute . . . "By the way," I said, "did you know you and I both made Mr. Blackwell's list?"

"Except, *I* was on his best-dressed list and *you* were on the worst," she said.

Nobody likes a bitchy princess, I thought, and added, "Meanwhile, honey, you had Princess Margaret on your list while I've got Demi and Madonna on mine. Princess, you're on the wrong list!" Then I snapped a Z in the air and marched away, until I reached the end of my train and could go no farther, since Diana was stepping on it (she's a size-ten shoe, at least). I tapped her broad, square shoulder, and pointed to her boat (I mean, foot), at which point she released me. Or at least that's the way the story went by the time I got onstage as a presenter and began my speech by simply saying, "Well, the queen of Queens got to meet the Princess of Wales!" The audience went nuts, and I became the belle of the ball!

It was truly a night to remember, and one they're still talking about. Upon finishing my speech, presenting the award, and briefly discussing the importance of supporting AIDS and breast cancer research, I went backstage and posed with Cynthia Rowley for a few photo ops and proceeded to leave. Just before I reached the exit, believe it or not, security from Harry Winston, the jewelers, stopped me and stripped me of my jewels. I couldn't believe they couldn't have waited until I had at least reached the limo, but this was the way it was done, and I exited from the theater naked. Thank God, Cynthia didn't expect the same with her dress, or I really would have given the paparazzi something to shoot!

As they whisked me away in the limo, I thought to myself, How mind-blowing it is, the people I've gotten to meet and the exotic places I've gotten to visit, all because of The Nanny. Yup, wherever I go, be it near or far, I forever and always feel like that gefilte fish out of water. But it is out of these situations that we get our material to write about.

Chapter 28

Traveling

You pay a dollar in Venice to have a hundred birds shit on you. No wonder they think Americans are stupid.

Now that I'm a celebrity, traveling to places is completely different, as are my needs. Like, we tend to stay at small hotels now for both the privacy and security factors. But what comes with small hotels, unless you're stayin' at a Circle 7 (always one of my parents' personal favorites), is a huge room tab. The most expensive place we had ever stayed cost . . . I don't even wanna say, it was so nauseating. Now, it did include alcohol, but honestly, we're Jewish . . . we're not a drinking people, so no bargain there . . .

It was Christmas in Vermont, right outta a picture postcard and near enough to New York, which is where we had to be on New Year's for my sister's wedding. The name of the place was Twin Farms, and I tell you it was a winter wonderland, but cold. Colder than even the word "cold" implies. This was Nanook of the north, my nose is gonna freeze off cold. We arrived and immediately sized it up as a low-key, old money kinda place. Not a nasal whine among 'em! A softspoken Englishwoman greeted us at the door and began to take us through the property and main house, which was where our suite was located.

"And this is the reading room, over here is our wine cellar, which we're very proud of, you can arrange for a private candlelit dinner down there if you like. We offer downhill private skiing, as well as cross country, ice skating, and a horse-drawn sleigh."

Just when she began to introduce a white-haired gentleman, I realized that my fly was open. Oh, Lord, why me? The car ride from New York was so long that I had unzipped my pants somewhere in Connecticut, and although I managed to snap them closed at the waist upon exiting from the car, I'd completely neglected the zipper.

As we entered our suite, it was a symphony of white and green toile. The wooden floors were heated, the bar was fully stocked as promised in the brochure, there were state-of-the-art TV, CD, and VCR. Even the bath products were nicer than anything I'd ever splurged on for myself at home. I mean, I've seen

Peter and me on our first tropical
vacation. Peter saw this after ten
years and said he'd never eat again.

Patty Duke, me, and Sean Astin about fifteen years
ago, when we met on vacation in Mexico. Wasn't he cute?

those clear-colored cubes of soap at the better drugstores. Each one is, like, five bucks! Well, after we touched everything, tried everything, and ordered everything (we needed a snack after that long drive), we both blossomed out with something that in no time at all turned into a flu.

Now, there we were, two kids from Queens, finally but grudgingly spending a king's ransom per night for the Christmas holiday to rival all others anywhere, bar none, and it became quite clear that we were not going to get to enjoy any of it. Of course, the management couldn't have been nicer or more understanding, not that the word *refund* was ever mentioned, but cold remedies, hot tea, fresh towels, and clean linens were provided constantly. Hour after hour, day after day, we watched the other guests enjoying our vacation from out of our bedroom window. And we're normally so helpless and hopeless, but under those circumstances we were absolutely pathetic.

"Hello, our fireplace went out again, could you help us? . . . We need more Evian, more tea bags, more tissues, more Nyquil . . ." You name it, we asked for it. We slept through Shangri-la. But out of all the amenities offered, the only one we

On the most expensive vacation we ever had, Peter and I had the flu.

Twin Dolphins in Mexico. To die for.

could still partake of was room service. And did we ever partake. We were gonna get our money's worth even if it meant eating ourselves to oblivion. And everyone was so accommodating, they served us our food by the course. We had no sooner finished the final course of the last meal than this poor little Asian woman was climbing the steps again with our mid-meal snack. By the time we checked out, we were completely recuperated and ten pounds heavier. As we drove off holding the basket of homemade goodies provided for the return trip home, we realized that we had had a once-in-a-lifetime experience. Having the flu *and* a full-time waitress.

Some trips require taking planes, but, unfortunately, Peter is a white knuckler, so it's always more intense an experience than necessary. God bless him, though, he goes, in spite of his fears. Once, on a small plane from Nantucket to Boston, the plane hit an air pocket, tipped sideways, and suddenly shook. Well, everyone got scared, but Peter did his best Tom Snyder impersonation and screamed, "Oh, my God, we're gonna crash," then realized quickly that he was the only one screaming and focused on me, who was trying to calm him but wore an expression like

You should've seen Peter white knuckling it when we were flying in that plane.

"Have you lost your MIND???" He turned to the little boy staring at him like he was nuts and said, "I'm not good in emergency situations."

Well, it was on a 747 to Tel Aviv that the pilot, who was a fan of *The Nanny,* invited us to sit with him and the copilot in the cockpit during the landing. Of course, I was game for the experience, but much to my surprise, Peter rose to the occasion as well. What he didn't admit until after having safely landed in Tel Aviv was that he went along just to make sure I didn't yak away to the pilots and distract them from flying the plane safely. Well, at least that made sense!

Peter panicking ...

But happy once he got to the food.

Being frisked was a good time had by all.

Me and Babs Bush petting
the dog, Millie.

Pete and Ron.

Miss Fine Goes to Washington

Visiting Babs and George Bush at the White House.

Peter meeting George Bush. But who's that blonde next to him?

Mashatu. We changed the name to mishbucha.

And you should have seen us on a photo safari in Botswana, there we were out in the bush tracking, of all things, an elephant. And let me tell you, those mothers are huge! It was me and Peter and my two cousins in a Jeep with Eric, our driver, and Congo, our tracker, plus a loaded rifle, which in many ways made me feel more nervous than secure. Well, it wasn't long before this elephant was getting annoyed with us for following him, and expressed this attitude quite clearly by rocking his head, flapping his ears, lifting his trunk, and screaming at us. Now, I can't stand upsetting an innocent animal but didn't want to be a pooper either, so I began touching up my lipstick and powdering my face because, needless to say, riding around in an open Jeep for hours with the dust and wind in your face does wonders for the complexion.

So after a minute or two of self-beautification, I noticed a sadistic glee in Eric's face as he stepped on the gas pedal in hot pursuit of this obese Pinocchio. "Eric," I said, "we've seen enough of the elephant, let's look for something else..." But Eric must get a kick out of scaring the tourists. After all, how much is there to do in Botswana for entertainment—see a lion, scare a tourist, the usual. He placated me and continued harassing this creature that to me was now taking on the look of a sumo wrestler or an irate Roseanne.

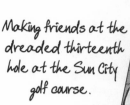

Making friends at the dreaded thirteenth hole at the Sun City golf course.

Faster and faster we bumped our way over the rugged bush country as Eric continued to say, "It's okay, no problem, man, he might lead us to the herd." Or he might stampede and squish us like bugs.

Absolute ecstasy, sitting on the terrace of the Villa San Michele overlooking Florence.

Peter and me in Portofino.

Peter pigging out on Italian room service.

A rare moment. All of us sitting at a table with no food on it.

Well, by now my sunglasses were covered with dust, my lip-stick was smeared all over my face, and the closest thing to a toi-let was this mashatu tree on the left. So I asked this miserable little bushman, who I regretted giving my autograph to, "Say, Eric, HOW DO YOU SAY in Botswanian, CUT THE CRAP OR NO TIP-O?" At which point he made a sharp left and we began photographing some timid, nervous creatures. Each other!

After the safari in Botswana we headed north to our next destination, the Holy Land. Israel was a trip. I've never been to a place where so many people speak on cellulars. Not even in L.A. is this practiced to quite such excess. We went on business with Robbie, Elaine, and Allan, but on one particular morning we decided to climb Masada (the mountain and ruins). My body-guard waited for us in the hotel lobby, as did my personal guide, but both were at opposite ends of the hotel lobby. Now, I usu-ally run about fifteen minutes late, and this morning was no different. Well, the tour guide was getting nervous and took out his cellular and called the bodyguard on his cellular.

"Where are they?!" he shouted.

This camel looked a lot better than he smelled.

"I don't know. Where are you? You're coming in very clear."

"I'm in the lobby."

"I'm in the lobby, too. Hang up, I'm coming over." He turned around and the other bodyguard was literally four feet away. Welcome to Israel.

When we approached Masada, Elaine and Allan caught one glimpse of the ambulance parked at the bottom of the moun-

Peter sure wasn't smiling once we reached the top.

While climbing Masada

tain and immediately informed everyone that they would meet us by the Dead Sea. The tour guide dropped us off and drove them on, then the bodyguard, who was a good sixty pounds overweight, said he'd take the tram up and meet us at the top. As far as he was concerned, I was on my own.

So Robbie, Peter, and I took the 3,000-foot climb up Masada on a 97-degree morning. We had fanny packs filled with survival gear that I acquired by cleaning out the hotel minibar. We each had an Evian and a box of Toblerone. We were the only ones on the snake path as we wound our way higher and higher. No one else in their right mind would attempt this climb much past dawn, but there we were at 10 A.M. in the full, blazing sun,

attempting the impossible. Well, by three quarters of the way up, Peter and I were stopping to rest every fifty feet. My face was beet red, and Peter could no longer form audible speech. I was certain I was having a heart attack and he a stroke. The water supply was getting low, and I wondered if a helicopter could somehow rescue us, but we persevered. Onward and upward went Robbie our leader, still in his twenties, mind you, slightly winded but clearly saddled with a couple of dead-beats.

Peter and me at the "schmilton" Hilton in Tel Aviv.

Peter, out of either guilt or embarrassment, waved Robbie on to go at his own pace, but I put a stop to that lunacy at once. "Are you nuts?" I asked while panting like a dog who's just realized he ran after a mechanical rabbit. "What if this turned into an emergency situation? He's gotta be the one to get help!"

Fran, I don't think I should have
had that last falafel.

Ocean
resturant

I guess he's not in the mood for
romance.

Robbie and me in Athens.

Finally we got to the top. I drowned myself under the water fountain and Peter was sitting, comatose, with his T-shirt seductively plopped on top of his head, when a woman who sold entry tickets to the ruins asked me if I was "the Nanny." "You are very big in Jordan. I love you too much!" Well, that recognition gave me the strength to powder my face and apply some lipstick in order to see the ruins with Robbie and take a picture in front of a three-foot mound of stone rubble that was the remains of the world's oldest synagogue. We then picked up Peter, who was passed out on a bench, and gingerly took the tram down.

It doesn't matter where I roam, I still remain the fish outta water. Even in Greece, my persona seemed to echo the bizarre. Lost in an economy car (the only automatic on the island of Santorini), we stopped at a gas station to ask directions to the airport. Not only hadn't anyone ever heard a voice sound quite

This is the texture of the sand in
Greece.

like mine, no one seemed to have a clue as to what I was asking, until finally I hung out of the car window, spread my arms like wings, and while tilting from side to side made a loud *vrroom* sound, which got my point across and was received with enthusiastic pointing and directing. As we sped off, I heard them all chattering something in Greek that ended with two simple words, "the Nanny."

Back Home

There's no place like home.

Two divas.

A drag queen's dream!

Chapter 29

If It's Friday, This Must Be Georgette Klinger

When did I become so high maintenance? I mean, I was always aware of my weight and the constant battle to keep it down, but the rest of me sorta looked after itself, barely taking my makeup off, rarely getting a manicure, and never coloring my hair. Those were my high school days through my twenties; now in my thirties, I do *everything*! And not to look different, but just to put everything back the way it used to be.

It ain't easy being a woman. Especially when we're led to believe almost nothing about us couldn't stand some improving. And sucker that I am, I buy into it lock, stock, and barrel. I mean, I've got a beauty regimen that gets applied with such precision NASA engineers have less to do. There's the basic washing and brushing, followed by skin bleach, acid-lotion pimple cream, sun block, lip balm, and makeup. And that's just the morning, at night there's a whole other sequence to the regime. I have become a slave to myself in the battle against time in which I am sure to lose. But what are my alternatives? Look like hell? No, thank you. So I plow ahead. Dutifully smearing sun block on the backs of my hands to avoid sunspots in future years, religiously getting my manicures and pedicures and courageously enduring those teeth-gritting waxings of unsightly body hairs from ankles to pits. Speaking of teeth, have you tried that new tooth-whitening kit that can only be pre-scribed by your dentist? What can I say? Honey, it works.

You should see me at a duty-free shop in an airport when they carry one of my obscenely priced miracle creams at 30 percent off. I stock up like I've found the fountain of youth itself. And, of course, living in L.A. doesn't help either, with its constant, year-round, glaring sun. Believe me, if it could turn a plum into a prune, just think what it's doin' to your face. I've pH-balanced, PABAed, and fruititioned myself up the wazoo.

Well, I no longer wear those trendy, old-fashioned wire-rimmed sunglasses anymore, I can tell you that much. Not since I began to notice the furrows in my forehead from all the gri-macing I was doing from the glare of the sun, because the shades I was using, though totally hip, were too small and com-pletely impractical. Now I wear wraparound frames that would make Jackie O's look like John Lennon's. Hey, it beats crow's feet, don't it?

One time, after a tiring season, Elaine and I booked our-selves into a luxurious health spa for women. This is the plus side to the beauty myth. Now, prior to our arrival we were requested to complete the guest questionnaire so the spa might better choose a program for each of us. Well, Elaine checked off that she was attending for the Fit 'N Trim program, while I, who could barely push the pen I was writing with, checked the box next to rest and renewal, aka have everyone else do everything for you. Well, clearly our paths would not cross too often over the course of a day, except on a few occasions.

Each morning Elaine took the 6:30 A.M. three-mile hike while I slept in bed. It was all so peaceful at this place and so effortless on every level. They even supplied clothes for you. Almost like a sleep-away camp for women with Gold Cards. We were given sweatsuits, shorts, T-shirts, kimonos, robes, sun hats, and visors, plus three meals a day, two snacks, different classes, beauty treatments and massages every day. As I ventured out to my first class of the day, tai chi (a slow, Chinese, dancelike series of motions), after enjoying a delicious breakfast in bed, I would pass Elaine, arms flailing, tits bouncing, as she painfully struggled through a step aerobics lesson. In contrast, the tai chi was quiet, methodical, slow. We were like the tortoise and the hare, weighing ourselves in at check-in and then heading our way toward that frighteningly honest scale at the finish, seven days later.

Next was my beauty treatment.

"Hi, Fran, I'm Carol, and I'll be giving you your beauty treatments this week," said this smiling blonde with the softest, gentlest voice.

Did everyone speak in whispers here? My voice seemed to carry and echo whenever I spoke, like the moo of a cow or the honk of a tugboat coming into harbor. But when she spread that almond-oatmeal honey scrub on my face, while my hands and feet, slathered in rich emollients, baked in electric warming mitts and booties, you could be sure my mouth was shut. When it was over, this angel actually brushed and braided my hair. This is heaven on earth.

As I floated toward the pool area, I could tell by the huge clamor of ladies clumped in one corner of the deck that the first snack had been served. Needless to say, it was easy to find Elaine in the sea of straw sun hats and purple gym wear. She always stood closest to the crudité and dip basket. A fistful of raw vegetables clenched within her fingers, cackling joyfully over the taste of the spicy cold vegetable broth that accompanied it. Poor Elaine set herself up the schedule of a masochist, so the snacks quickly became the highlight of her day.

We attended self-hypnosis, posture, cooking, and wreath-making (you never know when you may need it) classes. I have never felt more relaxed. And it was so sweet how everyone wore a uniform, just like bein' at one of those fancy boarding schools rich girls go to.

We felt like Tootie and Blair on *The Facts of Life*. Next, Elaine went on to huffing and puffing her way through circuit training while I meditated in yoga, followed by a nap period before lunch. I think Elaine, right about this time, was swimming laps in the pool. Finally lunchtime came, which we enjoyed together in my room, served to us on trays. It was always something satisfying: vegetable burrito, grilled shrimp salad, et cetera, but we nevertheless requested bread along with every meal. After lunch was when I took my scheduled walk of the day. We all had our schedules to follow, printed up by our very own guidance counselor on fan-shaped cards safety-pinned to our uniforms or the spa canvas bags we used instead of purses. Halfway through the week Elaine was referring to her counselor as "the Nazi" while I was blessing mine.

In the afternoons I had a one-hour massage in my room each day, after which I opted to rest and skip the second snack. But Elaine would've rather died, and proceeded to gorge herself on the fruit and fruit juice four-thirty combo. Needless to say, it wasn't long before Elaine complained of a gaseous stomach. Thank God, I'd brought Gas-X, because in no time she would be bloated up like the Goodyear blimp. I'll tell ya, this experience was the epitome of self-indulgent beautification, the culmination of every woman's quest for youth, beauty, and well-being. Now, what better way to demonstrate all this new knowledge but within the gift shop? There existed an oasis of products. All the nifty items used during each and every beauty treatment, video-tapes of tai chi, music to massage by, hair treatments, bath salts, candles, lotions, and sponges of every shape and size. And, of course, one didn't work without the others. What a paradise, and how primed we all were to spend, spend, spend. And we did, did, did!

On the last night the ladies, clad in kimonos, said their good-byes to their fast-made friends at the farewell dinner and listened to songs sung by the weight trainer. The next day Elaine and I, tucked away in the limo, sped off back to L.A. laden with our gift-shop merchandise, dried flower wreaths, and a lunch box filled with spa cuisine. God forbid we should get hungry on the drive home. When all was said and done, we each weighed three pounds less, and as we headed north on the San Diego Freeway, Elaine muttered that the next time she'd try the Rest 'N Renewal, too.

Chapter 30

Jack

Just when I thought my plate was full, something too good to resist came along. There I was, making the last entries in my book (this book), giving notes on a first-draft screenplay that Peter and I would produce in the spring of '96 with Caravan, as well as searching for a writer for the TriStar film we'll produce (do you believe this?), and coordinating my New York schedule to promote the third season of *The Nanny*, not to mention writing, producing, and acting in each episode.

Elaine called and said, "Honey, do I have a meeting for you. It's a film . . . directed by, you guessed it, Francis Ford Coppola." Oh, my God. Francis Ford *Godfather* Coppola. "It gets better," Elaine said. "It's for Disney, starring, of all people, Robin Williams!" Elaine needed a Librium, she was so hyper.

Wow, I wonder if Robin suggested me for this, or if it came to me some other way? Francis was only gonna be in L.A. a few days, and I had to work it into my schedule to meet him at once. Well, I was just getting over a terrible stomach flu and not really feeling my best, so I asked if somehow we could do it another day, or have him come to my house, I'd make a snack.

"Are you out of your mind?" Elaine said. "Get outta bed and go, go, go!" Elaine and Bob Gersh were having multiple orgasms over the importance of landing a role like this and wouldn't even entertain the idea of making any waves, so a meeting was set at an Italian restaurant of *his* choice for cocktails that very day.

"Honey, just jump in the shower and put on some makeup!" Elaine commanded.

"Oh, all right," I bellyached as I dragged my ass out of bed. The role wasn't a large one, but it was really juicy, and all my scenes would be with Robin. Oh, what a doll that Robin was for thinking of me, I thought. After all these years, too. We shoulda kept in touch. The part was the role of Dolores "D.D." Durante, a divorced mother of a ten-year-old who's thirty-five trying to look twenty-five. Oy, I'm never gonna get this, I'm sure it'll end up with more of a Mercedes Ruehl type, so I'll do what I always do when taking a power meeting for a role I'm totally wrong for: look gorgeous and hope that the director falls madly in love with me and someday hires me to play something more suitable.

Well, that's not exactly what happened. Somehow I managed to pull it together, set my hair, put on a face, and wear a stunning pants suit. Not bad for someone who was puking her guts up just a few hours earlier. As I entered the restaurant, the maitre d' greeted me. I informed him that I was to meet with Francis Ford Coppola and then wondered if I sounded stupid dropping all three of the man's names. "Right this way," he said, "I'll take you to Mr. Coppola's table."

The first person I laid eyes on was Cindy Crawford, aka the

ex–Mrs. Richard Gere and a supermodel in her own right. Well, there goes the part. "Cindy, hi!" I said as if I'd met a long-lost friend. I was just so excited to meet Cindy Crawford in person, I'm afraid I might have ignored Francis. Of course, we're on a first-name basis now. Well, Cindy, bless her warm heart, jumped out of her seat and gave me the biggest hug. Turns out she's a big fan of mine as well, and we both love to wear Todd Oldham's designs. There she was, one of the world's most famous beauties, the familiar mole over her upper lip, the thick mane of golden-brown hair, and *young*. Man, how could anyone be so rich, so gorgeous, and so young all at the same time?

Maintain confidence, I thought, you look damn good. And so what if she's like six two. What I lack in height I make up for with comic timing and business flair. Then Francis, who I guess was feeling somewhat left out of the equation, also stood up and asked the obvious question, "Do you two know each other?"

We both looked at him and simply said, "Nah."

Clearly it was time to start payin' attention to Francis and Fred Roos, the man who's cast all of Coppola's films since *American Graffiti,* so I slid my way onto the banquette, ordered a bottle of Evian, and began to converse with Coppola, but found my eyes panning over to Cindy. God, what a flawless complexion. I wonder what kinda base she uses? I thought to myself as Francis began going on about how this week was about meeting all the people that he recently thought he'd like to meet, whether they were right for the movie or not. By now my competitive edge was kicking in, and, well, I could practically taste this part.

It turned out that Cindy was attending the same AIDS benefit I was in a couple of days, so we promised to connect there, at which point she had to leave and gracefully said her good-byes to Francis, Fred, and me. Now it was my turn, or should I say, his turn. I focused on this man, this genius, this star maker, and liked him at once. He was sweet, warm, and amiable. He laughed when I said something funny, and seemed to enjoy his life tremendously. He had the familiar dark hair and beard, salted with patches of gray, glasses, and a bright Hawaiian shirt. Basically a very unassuming guy.

He talked about his vineyard in Napa Valley, his lodge in Belize, as well as several other properties, and while his mouth moved all I could hear was the voice in my head repeating, "None live as the rich," a Fitzgerald quote that resonated like a deafening echo. Boy, I always thought Danny and Donna were loaded, but this guy lives in a whole other stratosphere.

I said that I was curious to know how this meeting came about. I mean, it's not like the Coppolas of the world are breaking down the doors for sitcom stars, so I asked him, "Was it Robin?"

"You know Robin?" he asked innocently.

Now I'm thinking, So it wasn't Robin. Well, I'm glad we didn't keep in touch. So would it be a good thing if I now tell him I was already in a film with Robin (a flop, I might add), or not? . . . Oh, what the hell.

"Actually, we worked together a few years ago in a film called *Cadillac Man*. I played one of his girlfriends."

"Oh, I forgot he did that movie," he said.

Yeah, you and everybody else, I thought. Well, if it wasn't Robin, then who? How? I mean, my agents are good, but no one was rushing to take the credit for this major coup.

"It came from me," this adorable, cuddly bear of a man confessed. "You know, I never watch TV, so I had no awareness of you or your successful series . . ." Well, that I could have lived without hearing, I thought, as he continued. "But I was staying in a hotel somewhere, I got back late, and for some strange reason decided to turn on the set. That was when I saw your appearance on Conan O'Brien's show . . ." Well, if this didn't take the cake. Of all the odds, for this master filmmaker, who never watches TV, to turn on the tube and see me on, of all shows, *Late Night with Conan O'Brien*. "You were so warm, so funny, so beautiful, sexy, natural. I said right then, 'I must meet this actress.'" I squealed and giggled from his praises. "Of course, I didn't remember your name or what you'd done, I'd never seen you before," he pontificated.

All right, already, with the "you've never seen me before." This was bordering on insulting. I mean, how much of a vacuum can a person live in, I thought, but simply said, "Go on." He did.

"All I could say when I returned to my office was the way you looked and [here it comes] your laugh." Then he proceeded to do his best foghorn impersonation, and based on that, Fred Roos knew it was me. I swear, I booked myself on *Conan O'Brien* the next day, just because I felt so indebted.

In fact, I did the *Conan* show and told him the whole story, to which Conan said that I owed him. I said I'd give him a blow job after the show, and the audience went nuts. He said, "Well, let's hurry up and get this show over with."

Back to Cope! We started talking about the role of D.D., which by now I wanted so bad I could taste it. "Well, I know the character is probably much tackier than I appear to be," I said as I found myself unconsciously cleaning under my fingernail with the edge of a matchbook.

"I see the character as pretty," he said.

Praise glory! He sees the character as bein' pretty. If I couldn't have done an Irish jig right there and then. Turns out, we both grew up in the same neighborhood in Queens and reminisced about everything from Union Turnpike to the soft-serve ice cream parfaits at the old and now gone Gertz department store in Jamaica, Queens. Finally, I felt it was time to draw the meeting to a close. Don't overstay your welcome, I always say. Besides, if I had one more sip of Evian, my bladder was gonna burst.

"I feel like you're my coup, because *I* found you, not Fred."

Please, please, let's not fight over who gets the credit, what say we just offer me the part already, I thought, but out loud only laughed.

"We'll walk you out," he said gallantly as we all headed for the door. Oh great, now I can't even stop to take a leak before leaving. I mean, what was I to do, ask Francis Ford Coppola to stand outside the ladies' room and wait for me? So I just held it in until I got back home.

The very next day, Fred Roos called and requested footage from *Cadillac Man* and *The Nanny*. Along with that I also sent a case of croutons. Cindy may be gorgeous, but I got stale bread on my side! It seemed like we were gonna find out right away, but by the time I caught up again with Cindy at the AIDS benefit, I still had not heard.

"Did you get the Coppola film?" she asked.

Oh, how I wish I could have just said yes, but could only answer, "They said I'm their first choice, but so far nothing." Oh, if that didn't sound pathetic. If I was the first choice, they would have booked me already, and being that they hadn't, I must, in reality, assume that I hadda be the second choice. Or no choice at all.

Well, life rolled merrily along anyway. Working on the book, the screenplay, and, of course, *The Nanny*. Each day performing the timely task of coordinating my busy schedule in New York, where I'd go to promote the third-season fall premiere during my one-week hiatus in September. Every minute was accounted for, from filming a commercial to taping *David Letterman*. When, wouldn't ya know it, from out of the blue they book me on the Coppola film and request my presence at a rehearsal for the same week as my New York trip. Oy. Cancel the theater tickets, cancel *Regis & Kathie Lee*, cancel my CBS box seats for the U.S. Open men's semifinals. Crowd everything that's left into the back end of the week, because before I get to New York I first have to fly to Napa Valley for the rehearsal of *Jack*, Coppola's movie.

We taped *The Nanny* on a Friday, Saturday we worked on the feature that we were developing, and Sunday we flew to San Francisco. An enormous black stretch limo met us at the airport and drove us up to Napa. It was a beautiful drive, vineyard after vineyard full with grapes hanging from their delicate vines. We settled into the Auberge du Soleil. A gorgeous Relais & Châteaux hotel set high above the valley, with the most breathtaking views and the most delicious cuisine. Everyone else was being put up at the Marriott, but if I was already in Napa, let it be at the Auberge. I didn't care if I had to lay out a few bucks, what do I work so hard for anyway, right?

We had a wonderful, relaxing afternoon and evening that Sunday, and the next morning a car picked me up to take me to the Coppola estate. Again, this embarrassingly long limousine arrived, and I left, leaving Peter behind to enjoy that paradise known as the Auberge. As we turned into the entry to Coppola's estate, formerly the Inglenook winery, I watched out the window as acres of vineyard rolled by. The private road led to a grand white Victorian mansion. By this point my nose was pressed against the limousine window like a kid outside a candy store. As we continued past the lush, green rolling lawns, the pool, the stables, the babbling brook, we drove over a small wooden bridge and parked in front of an old barn that Francis had converted into a rehearsal hall.

Standing around out front were a bunch of ten-year-old boys (actors in the movie), Robin, Francis, Bill Cosby, Diane Lane, and Brian Kerwin, plus a few odd assistants, mothers, and the caterer (I sniffed *him* out immediately). Now, I make it a policy, when attending work-related events such as this, to dress in some way resembling the character. "Leave nothing to the imagination" is my motto. The driver walked around the back of the car to open my door. By now all eyes were locked on the sight of this tranquil farm setting with this vulgar, incongruous pimp-mobile parked on a winding, country dirt road. As the driver opened the door, I stepped out, one foot at a time.

There I stood in my Stephan Kelian spike-heeled slides, designer jeans, black lace bra, and mesh T-shirt. Why me, Lord?

Well, Fran, hold your head up, walk tall, and act like nothing's strange or weird whatsoever. As I maneuvered my way over a wooden planked bridge and dirt and straw path, my heels wobbled with every step I took, until finally my heel got stuck between planks. One of the kids pulled it out for me. "Thanks, honey." Okay, take a deep breath, and whatever you do, don't trip! All the boys gave me a big hello. I guess they recognized me as "the Nanny." Robin was trying to remain in character, and although cordial, he was a bit cool, as well.

Anyway, I entered the barn, and Francis grabbed me and gave me a big hug. Bill Cosby was dictating some complex instructions to the caterer on how he likes his cappuccino. I took some fruit and half a bagel and moved into the main hall. Well, we all went around the room and introduced ourselves. Then we read the screenplay out loud. It seemed to go well. Okay, is it over? I wondered. Can I go back to the hotel now?

But as luck would have it, Francis announced to the company that it was time to play theater games! Oh boy, oh boy, oh boy. "Everybody out in the road," he shouted.

Wait a minute. What road? That dusty dirt and straw road? There I was in a circle of actors throwing an imaginary ball and following protectors while escaping enemies. I was so inappropriately dressed, I wanted to die. But I must say on my own behalf that I didn't let it get me down. On the outside I threw myself into the exercise with the best of 'em as the leather weave on my shoe began to cake with dust. And a blister started to surface on my right toe.

Afterward I briefly spoke to Diane Lane, a beautiful-looking woman and quite thin, I might add. "Diane, you recently had a baby?" I asked, conversationally.

"She's two," she answered.

"You seem so thin, did it take you a long time to knock off the weight, or did it happen right away?" I asked with interest. Not being a mother myself, there's not a whole lot I know on the subject of children and raising a family, but the subject of postpartum weight reduction happens to be one I'm always curious about.

"No, I got thin almost immediately; twenty-eight days later I was shooting a film," she answered with perkiness.

"I take it you're not Jewish" was all I could say.

I talked to Francis about the character's look, and he liked my suggestion of wearing a space between my teeth. "I find a space between the teeth very sexy," he said (when it came time to shoot we opted to lose the space), and also liked the idea of D.D. working as a cocktail waitress on the lunch shift at the Beef & Brew, serving up drinks to local businessmen. That meant I could wear my uniform in the first scene where I leave work to meet with the principal (Robin), and I loved that idea.

The first time you meet this lady, before I even say word one, you know what she does, how much she earns, her probable level of education, and that she's devoted to her son. That's a lot of information to learn by one simple device, and that's especially helpful in getting to know D.D. in a limited amount of screen time. I did improvs with the kid and the teacher, improvs with the kid and Robin, improvs alone with Robin, and they all went really well, if I do say so myself. And even if I don't, others did, so I was pleased.

But by now the heels were diggin' into the sides of my feet like two chain saws, and I really couldn't wait to take a Jacuzzi at the hotel. I was overworked to begin with, so even rehearsing with such great talents could not keep my body from longing for a nice hot bath. Needless to say, when Francis announced that he was cooking dinner and we were all invited, I was a little less than enthusiastic. Who would have thought I would turn down a dining invitation to Francis Ford Coppola's? Instead, I hobbled into my 200-foot black stretch limousine, went back to the hotel, took a hot bath, and soaked my tootsies in my favorite Roots Balsamic Bath Oil that I am never without, then watched the premiere episode of the third season of *The Nanny,* followed by a candlelit dinner with my husband on the balcony of the hotel dining room. Of course, Peter and I managed to fight through our appetizers over his favorite pastime, monitoring my food, but managed to make up once *he* apologized just about the time our entrées were served. An otherwise perfect day . . .

When I flew up to San Francisco to shoot my scenes in *Jack*, we decided to stay in town. "We" being me and Peter, Chester, and, of course, Robbie. Shooting would take place both in and around the "City by the Bay," so we booked ourselves into the Sherman House, another example of a perfect, small Relais & Châteaux hotel. When we were shown our room, it was a large, magnificently decorated suite done in dark, heavy, Jacobean style furnishings. The bay window was just that. A window looking out to the bay, the Golden Gate Bridge, and Alcatraz.

"What, no terrace?" I questioned, wondering what we would do with Chester when he's gotta go but we don't want to. As Robbie checked out the smaller window, Peter was already in the club chair, television remote in hand.

"There's a fire escape out this window, will that do?" asked Robbie, who was already picturing this dog-walking issue as becoming his responsibility.

I looked out the window and saw a small platform with a ladder. "That'll do," I said, much to Robbie's relief, as I gingerly picked up Chester and put him out to take a leak. We had officially arrived . . .

Robin Williams is such a doll. I love working with him.

The first few days were spent shooting the barroom brawl scene. It's also where I have to kiss Robin for the first time in the movie, but obviously not for the first time. I hadn't worked with him since *Cadillac Man,* but there was an instant comfort, familiarity, and ease to our scene work. Robin told Peter and me a story about *Cadillac Man* that we'd never heard before.

Apparently, a guy stole a car in Manhattan and drove the vehicle over the 59th Street bridge and smack dab into the center of a scene in the film that happened to include about three hundred extras all dressed in SWAT-team uniforms. Well, the thief thought they were real and got so scared at such a sight that he stopped the car, stepped out with his hands in the air, and started screaming, "Don't shoot! I did it!" True story.

Robin is the gentlest, most caring man to work with and for. He and Dan Aykroyd are my mentors on how a star should behave with regard to cast and crew. Couple that with the kind, jovial warmheartedness of Francis and you've got a great, relaxed work experience. After having seen the footage of the car scene I had with Robin, Francis pulled me off to the side and went on and on about how wonderful it had turned out.

"You're so accessible, were you always like this, or did the series help bring it out? Sometimes I have to work so hard to get an actor's performance, but you, Fran, make my job so easy, you do one thing, and then if I ask something else of you, you do that, too!"

Ah, does life get any better than this, I thought, but found myself pitching "The Beautician and the Beast" to him for a

Hugging Francis Ford Coppola. I loved him, he loved me. Does life get any better than this?

spring shoot in Italy. God forbid I should miss an opportunity, but meanwhile the man actually seemed interested.

After a lovely visit to the Williamses' home one Sunday afternoon, we went to enjoy the sunset from the terrace of the Alta Mira Hotel in Sausalito. Incidentally, Robin and Marsha's home has the most incredible views of the bay. I should think one could travel to the ends of the earth and not see a view more magnificent than theirs. The whole house has a whimsical, magical feel to it and seems quite suitable as a backdrop for an imagination as special as his. Their children are warm and relaxed, and I complimented them, as I believe a sweet child reflects well on the parents. As Marsha walked me from room to room, explaining the changes she'd made and the walls she'd broken down, we entered one with a couch that was covered with stuffed toy gorillas of varying sizes and expressions.

"For some reason, people always send us stuffed toy gorillas," Marsha said.

"Do you think it's because Robin's so hairy?" I asked innocently, but realized at once that I'd made a teeny-weeny faux pas.

She took a beat, looked at me, and said, "No . . . I . . . don't . . ."

Whoopsie. Did I say a no-no? But something told me she was actually considering this possibility, since up until then there had been no other explanation.

Meanwhile, Peter got one look at the remote-control station in Robin's entertainment room and got sucked into that black hole for half the tour. We said our good-byes and drove off to the Alta Mira. Now, the view from the terrace overlooks the bay and the city, which I reveled in while sipping a glass of white wine, but Peter was far more intrigued by the wedding reception going on on the other half of the terrace. It was a Jewish wedding, there were yarmulkes everywhere and a band playing the hora. He even stole an hors d'oeuvre from a passing waiter.

It was like I was a fly on the wall, being there without having to wear high heels and support hose. We sat and watched as the city went from dusk to a million twinkling lights, and then decided to move on, when who stopped us in the lobby on her way to the ladies' room but Lillian Luhrman, the mother of the groom. Lillian apparently was a big fan and zeroed right in on me.

"Oh, my God, 'the Nanny,' oh, I never miss your show, come with me, you must meet my son." And she grabbed my hand and schlepped me back out to the wedding, stopping along the way to introduce me to one son or another. "I have five children, three doctors and three lawyers."

"Um . . . wait a minute," I said, "if you've got five children, how could ya have three doctors and three lawyers?"

"One's both!" she exclaimed. Three out of the four sons I met didn't own a TV (Lillian, this isn't doing much for my ego), but the photographer grabbed a picture of me and Lil for the album anyway.

Well, Peter managed to steal a week and a half away from *The Nanny*, but eventually he had to return to the writers' room to work on the script I would come back to upon completion of my work on *Jack*. Elaine was his replacement. Unfortunately, she arrived in time for the high school graduation scene, one that involved three hundred extras and massive crane shots, which take forever to set up and usually leave the talent to long and boring waiting fests in their trailers. Well, there sat Elaine, knitting away in my trailer while bitching about the bad cellular reception we were having on our mountain location, when an assistant director knocked on our trailer door requesting Chester for a shot in the movie.

"You're kidding?" I asked, but was already brushing his coat and spraying his breath.

"We have a pan shot that starts with Robin's feet, and we'd like a small dog to walk through the shot to create a little interest. What do you think?" the assistant director asked meekly, as if imposing, but I paid no notice as I quickly rolled the sleeves on Chester's little sweatshirt.

"Oh, that sounds great." Yeah, I could really see the whole

Chester and me resting between takes of his big moment in "Jack."

thing, oh, boy, Chester and Robin together again in a movie. "Can Robbie be the one to walk him?" Every bone in my back-stage mother's body was turned on, that is, unless it meant that I had to move or anything. She said Robbie would be fine, and the three of them left to shoot the scene.

The rehearsal went great, Robbie later said. Chester, while walking past Robin's feet, stopped for a brief but dramatic pause, smelled the sneaker, and then continued on his way. "Perfect, let's shoot it exactly the same way, don't change a thing," shouted the director. And so it began. Take after take of Robin's feet, Robbie's feet, and Chester walking across but never stopping for the moment when he would sniff the shoe. On the last take, Chester gave the performance of his life. It was all there. The nuances, the gestures, that touching and beautifully understated pause, and then the sniff and, alas, the exit. Sheer poetry. They all applauded, and for the rest of the day the whole company was talking about my dog, the genius. It was a proud day, I can say that.

When Elaine left for La La Land, my girlfriend Judi came up for a couple of nights on a business/pleasure trip. It was fun being just the two of us. Over the eighteen years we've been friends, we've shared bad things like the break-in, good times on vacations and holidays. She's had two husbands, and to date, four engagements, but through the years our friendship and

Judi came up to visit and so did Todd.

mutual love has remained the one constant.

For exercise we took Chester and marched up the steepest part of Fillmore. Two steps at a time we huffed and puffed our way to the top, kidding ourselves into thinking that if only we lived here, we'd do this every day. Suddenly Chester decides he needs to take a dump and begins to squat right there on the sidewalk. Well, that really wasn't the worst part, since I brought a tissue for just such an event and was fully prepared to scoop Chester's poop, but what I wasn't prepared for was that as each turd plopped from his butt to the ground, it would begin to roll down the steps of this mountain San Franciscans euphemistically call a sidewalk. What a sight, there I was chasing dog turd as it defiantly rolled away. As I got close, it rolled under a moving car to its demise. Oh, well, I tried. So much for exercise, let's get a cappuccino.

The last time I got to spend some quality time with Judi was when we were both in New York on business about six weeks earlier. That week it was both Judi's and my sister Nadine's birthday, so to celebrate I got theater tickets for the Broadway shows *Company* and *Sylvia*. Peter and I invited Nadine to see *Sylvia* because it was a highly touted comedy about a dog named Sylvia, and since Nadine's not too big on musicals, we saved Sondheim for Judi. Well, if that wasn't ever a wrong way to go. Little did I know, but at the end of the play, Sylvia the dog dies, and the owners eulogize her to the audience. When I glanced over at Nadine (who, incidentally, had very recently put her poodle, Missy, to sleep after seventeen years), she was hysterically crying, face as red as a beet, mascara running black tears down her cheeks. "Happy birthday, Nay . . ." Well, how was I supposed to know the dog dies in the end?

Well, just so my streak didn't break and I remained two for two, Judi's night at the theater ended in tears as well. The central character in *Company* is a friend of all the couples', someone who's miserable when in a relationship yet always longs to find one when he's out of a relationship. Now, Judi, who is questioning her current relationship, identified with the internal struggle of this character; for her it was like looking in a mirror. At the Italian restaurant we went to afterward, the waiters all brought out a birthday cake with a single candle for our friend Judi, who wept pitifully through a six-waiter chorus of "Happy Birthday to You."

Well, Judi's fiancé, Rick, showed up in San Francisco on Saturday, so that night Robbie and I took a stretch limousine to the Bridge School benefit concert at the Shoreline Amphitheater in Mountain View. We got tickets and backstage passes through the publicist on *Jack*. Our experience backstage was awesome. I regretted, though, not having worn my hair like Bobbi Flekman of *Spinal Tap* so all the rock stars would have known who I was. But as it was, I walked right up to Bruce (the Boss) Springsteen as he waited in the wings of the stage for his intro.

"Hi, Bruce, Fran Drescher. We said at the House of Blues, next time we run into each other we should say hello."

When I sat next to Bruce at one of the opening-night parties at the L.A. House of Blues that Danny Aykroyd hosted, Bruce had mentioned that he once took an elevator with me, to which I had responded, "Stop it, you knew who I was and didn't say anything? Ya hadda know I was plotzing to say something, but didn't want to intrude on your space." We were both staying at the same hotel and had gotten in the same elevator. Peter and I were pinching each other, trying to remain cool yet acknowledge the fact that we were riding in an elevator with the Boss.

Oh, he looked great at this concert, and he recognized me at once and with that really adorable crooked smile he said, "I was just watching you the other night."

"Where, on *The Nanny*?" I asked like an idiot, as if I'm in a million things or something. But he was solid, confident, and said, "Of course," with a chuckle. "How's ya wife, Patty?" I asked.

"She's home getting the kids ready for Halloween . . . I'll be flying back right after this."

God, what a guy, and a family man to boot. Boy, whatever gave me the impression that he was short; he's not short at all, or at least not to me he wasn't. I turned to Robbie, who was patiently standing just slightly behind me, and brought him into the circle and introduced Bruce Springsteen to Robbie Schwartz. As Robbie reached to shake Bruce's outstretched hand, all he could say was, "It's an honor."

All in all, *Jack* turned out to be one of the great and satisfying experiences in my career. Working with the best and having them love you is the greatest feeling. Francis is soft-toned and even-tempered, he rules with a gentle touch and runs a loose and relaxed set. The whole time I worked on the movie he was negotiating for the purchase of a private jet *and* trying to diet. Just vegetables and carbohydrates for lunch.

"I'm being so good on my diet," he bragged like a good little boy.

"What do you need to diet for?" I said. "You're already a king!"

To which the great Coppola responded, "Yeah, but I'd like to be a thin king!"

Chapter 31

The Days of Whine
and Toes-es

Peter and I generally have a lot on our minds and have difficulty sleeping. We actually spent—I won't tell you, it's so obscene—a king's ransom on an electric bed from Duxiana, the synonym for "sucker" when you're handed your receipt. The bed does everything but feed us, and it is sooo comfortable, but still, sleeping through the night is a rarity, and we almost always pop out of bed by 7:15 A.M. Peter flips on the TV with his remote control before uttering his first word (I tell ya, I should only get the attention he shows that remote), I slip into my robe and slippers and head toward the bathroom, when Ramon and Angelica arrive.

They are our house couple and handle most of the chores around the house. In the beginning, when we first started using them, they would work one afternoon every other week, then, as I began to work more, I had them once a week, then three times a week, and now, with our twenty-five-hour schedules and eight-day weeks, they come five days a week, which is absolute heaven. They do everything for us from daily cleaning, cooking, marketing, and gardening to runs to the dry cleaner's and pet groomer's.

"Desea desayuno?" whispers Angelica through our bedroom door, to which I respond, *"Si, si."* I would like breakfast. Within minutes, she enters with a tray. Peter takes the morning *Times* and eats his cereal. Still in bed, with it now bent into a sitting position (it vibrates, too; now, if it could only drive us to work), TV remote in hand, he chomps on his Nutri-Grain, flipping away.

An hour later, we enter the studio lot, the gate guard waves us on, and we park in Peter's spot. Robbie meets us at the car, no longer my assistant but now my associate producer. He

The "A" team.

books me in after rehearsal for an edit/notes session of last week's latest show cut. Peter takes the dog into his office as I advance toward the soundstage for rehearsal. I pass Frank and Diane smokin' on the porch outside the writers' room and wave good morning. They cough back, "Good morning."

There is an unquenchable thirst for jokes and more jokes on a show like *The Nanny*, and Peter and I set a very high standard for the level and quality of joke that we'll let pass. All too often, TV sitcoms underestimate their viewership and allow for soft, mediocre comedy to dominate an episode. Not us . . . So, till ya find writers who will rise to the occasion, it's like finding a needle in a haystack.

Besides Rob, Pru, Peter, and me (whom I refer to as the "A" team), we owe much of *The Nanny*'s success to writer/co-executive producer Diane Wilk and writer/supervising producer Frank Lombardi and their endless ability to pitch. Not baseballs, but jokes. They are both absolute riots, as colorful in their personalities as the characters they write. And the energy of each of them. It could be midnight and they're still goin' strong. Peter calls these people his joke machines. Each has the voice of the show perfectly, pitching jokes for all characters

Frank and Diane. Don't ever leave me!

equally as well. These two are the only cigarette smokers in the room, so they're forced to step outside the bungalow like two kids cutting class as they puff smoke like chimneys and pitch ideas through the open window.

Once Peter and I returned from a weekend getaway and raved about the hotel, which caught Diane's ear. Unfortunately, we gave her the wrong hotel name and realized it only after Diane was already off on her romantic getaway with her husband, Doug. Oy. When Monday morning came round, Diane's head was outside the window, huffing and puffing her More cigarette. Peter overheard her accusing us of not having any taste in hotels. Poor Diane, we had accidentally recommended Rancho del Rio, a golf resort for retirees, surrounded by convalescent homes, somewhere near San Diego. Unfortunately, the incredible place where we stayed was the Rancho Valencia. Peter had to face the music. He entered the writers' room smiling. Diane did a slow burn.

"Great hotel, huh?"

She's funny even when she's upset.

Stop eatin', Val.

We couldn't help but laugh and took Diane and Doug to dinner one night to make up for it. Well, sorta. I got sick at dinner and had to leave to throw up. Don't ask.

Frank's hysterical, too. He gets so excited when he's pitching a joke that he will often flip over in his chair, which is usually precariously perched on two legs. To call Frank a klutz is an understatement, but it's so funny each time he falls, it always cracks up the room. Once he was outside smoking when he shoved his face against the window screen to pitch a joke, then quite abruptly dropped out of view, followed by a loud thump and a loud "OWWW!"

"What happened??" we all shouted. The entire room went silent and looked at the window.

After a long beat, we heard, "I'm okay, I'm okay. Don't look. I just fell off the porch!"

Frank and Diane are the backbone of our show, and I hope they stay writing for *The Nanny* for as long as we're on the air! Or I might have to recommend to Diane another fabulous resort.

Now the *Oprah Winfrey* people were doing a show in which they would play matchmaker for some eligible person chosen by a celebrity and asked if I would do it. Well, it seemed harmless enough, and who would be a better candidate than Robbie Schwartz? So the *Oprah* people came later that day to tape Robbie at work on *The Nanny* and tape me with Robbie telling the audience why I think he is such a great catch. It was fun.

"Robbie needs a woman who's ambitious, attractive, and funny, but I'm already married . . ." I said, attempting to amuse.

He adds, "She definitely has to have a great sense of humor."

"Meanwhile," I interject, "that gorgeous blonde you met in South Africa never cracked a joke once!" to which Robbie responds, "*She* could have been a vegetable, I wouldn't have cared!"

Well, the *Oprah* people seemed pleased, packed up their equipment, and went home. In a few weeks, Robbie will fly to Chicago to appear on the *Oprah Winfrey* show and meet his

"Victor, Victoria," watch out!

Darrell McIntyre did the makeup, and Dugg Kirkpatrick received an Emmy nomination for the hair.

There's me as a man. Can you believe how much Howie and I look like brothers?

I grab Charlie and do this as often as possible.

blind date. Somehow, I've told him, we've got to figure out a way to use this experience on *The Nanny*. Like everything else. Meanwhile, the kid gets his fifteen minutes of fame!

Later that day, Dorothy, God bless her, was running a good hour and a half ahead of schedule, so the talent prepared for a pre-shoot, which is usually a part of a scene or an entire scene that requires some special effect that could not be done in front of a live audience because of the time factor.

Well, this afternoon Charlie will shoot part of the elevator scene, where he and Miss Fine get stuck in it together. However, I will be in my trailer giving Robbie my edit notes on last week's show (we're always working on last week's, this week's, and next week's shows all at the same time) while all this takes place, since Charlie will be working with my stunt double in the pre-shoot.

She will hang from the ceiling and dangle her feet in Mr. Sheffield's face until she eventually falls through, just as Maxwell declares that he wouldn't know the right woman for him if she fell from the sky. On Friday I'll tape the upper-body stuff in the shaft of the elevator, above the ceiling from which the stuntwoman hangs.

Well, there I was, stretched out on the couch in my trailer dictating notes to Robbie, who sat on the club chair with the script, remote control in one hand and pen in the other, when I said to Robbie, "Turn on the feed [the in-house channel], and lemme see what this elevator stuff is looking like!" Now, bear in mind that Peter sits with Dorothy in the control booth while the taping goes on, or they work on the stage, giving direction to the talent. Rob and Pru were already long gone for the day, off on this night to some Clinton fund-raiser.

Suddenly, my TV switches off the tape and over to Channel 60, and there I see for the first time my stunt double, a dark-haired, round-faced woman approximately my size and shape, wearing the Gianfranco Ferré evening gown that I will wear tomorrow, hanging by her waist from the ceiling with her feet dangling, while Lisa, my stand-in, reads the lines that I will per-form on Friday. Then I saw it with my very own eyes . . . A BUNION! This stuntwoman, who was supposed to be doubling for *me,* had a bunion on her right foot. A bunion and a weird-looking pinkie toe as well. "Call the control booth," I shouted to Robbie. "That woman's got a bunion!"

When Frances in the booth picks up the phone, I say to her, "Lemme see a close-up of her feet. Yeah, her feet!" Suddenly my entire TV screen is filled with this poor stuntwoman's feet, and there it is, as clear as day, a bunion the size of a walnut sticking off the side of her foot. "Oh, my God," I whine, "get some makeup, do something, I'm supposed to be a sex symbol for God's sake. My double can't have *facrimpta* [crooked] feet!"

By this point, Robbie, me, and Jay were laughing hysterically at the absurdity of this situation as Dorothy now gets on the phone, saying calmly, "Dear, it's Dorothy, dear. Now we all think it looks good. What are you suggesting, we bring in a makeup person and reshoot the entire scene again?"

"Well, she's got a bunion and this pinkie toe that's really weird lookin'—" I try to explain.

"Dear, dear," Dorothy interjects, "why don't you take a look at what we've got in the can and then we'll decide what needs to be done."

Just as we hang up the phone, it rings again. It's my mother. "I'm very worried about Nadine. Ever since she came home from that Club Med vacation in Haiti she hasn't felt well—"

I immediately interject, because I've been on the receiving end of a conversation with my mother when she's obsessing about my sister, "Ma, Ma, I gotta call ya back, we're right in the middle of a bunion crisis here on the set," and just as if I'd said the sky is blue she says, "All right, call me when it's over."

So me and Robbie marched ourselves out of the trailer and into the control booth off the soundstage where Peter and Dorothy, among others, awaited our arrival. You know, I kinda assumed her feet would be *nicer* than mine, I never considered they could be worse! Well, it didn't take the room long to see things my way. I mean, once pointed out, it was difficult not to focus on that bunioned, broken-pinkied, hammertoed monstrosity of a foot. But what were we to do besides laugh, as these hanging feet were completely unsuspecting of the microscope through which they were now being scrutinized.

"Shall we try putting her in a pair of hose? Perhaps that will soften this hideous sight?" asked Dorothy, and then we all cracked up again.

Peter, who's checking the clock and getting nervous, looks at me and shouts, "Do you want us to put her in panty hose or should you do it?"

"Me? I'm gonna hang from the ceiling for the entire scene, are you nuts? Do you want me to throw my back out? With all that I have to do! . . . Let's try the hose. If it doesn't work, I'll climb up."

As we sat in the control booth watching the monitor, within seconds we were seeing Brenda running into the shot, pushing panty hose up the feet of those flailing legs, still completely unaware of the hysteria incurred by the sight of this atrocity we euphemistically call a foot.

By now we are rolling from laughter as Brenda forces the hose up the dangling legs, and I get another brainstorm. Tell Charlie to try discreetly as much as possible to hide that damned bunion. So, as the cameras roll again to reshoot the scene with the stuntwoman in hose, there's Charlie, God bless him, desperately trying to look casual as he continually grabs at her bunion. Well, all I

That's me copping another feel from Charlie. Is he delicious or what?

can say was that the hose squished the pinkie toe together with the others and managed to make it more uniform, and thanks to Charlie camouflaging the bunion, I never had to climb up there myself. Boy, I haven't laughed that hard in a long time. I'll tell ya, there are moments when it's all just so absurd you gotta laugh if ya wanna keep your sanity! P.S., when we showed the pre-shoot to the audience on tape night, several people commented that the feet coulda done more, and those bunions! Needless to say, a reshoot using my feet is scheduled right after my pedicure next Thursday.

The craziest part of all was that there was this E! channel crew following me around to cover me while functioning as a producer for their special on powerful women. Yes, I'm so powerful I've become a bunion inspector. Typical Fran, what can I say?

I called my mother back and patiently listened to her go on and on about my sister Nadine's intestinal problems. "Well, we'll know more

A scene from "The Nanny." After a food fight.

when the tests come back," I said placatingly, and ran out before the stores closed to see if I could find a pair of shoes for this new pants suit I was to wear to an event. Well, I managed to make it to Barneys in time to pick out a pair of Manolo Blahniks. Then, while standing at the pay desk, I was approached by one of the shoe saleswomen.

"I love you, and I've seen every talk show you've ever been on, and you were so great in *My Cousin Vinny*—" HELLO!

And that wasn't the first time I was mistaken for Marisa Tomei, her and Laura San Giacomo. I was at a Dustin Hoffman–hosted fund-raiser for summer camp for terminally ill children once when a group of campers surrounded me, telling me how great I was, and naturally I think they're talking about me until one of them says how great I was in *Pretty Woman*. I signed all their autograph books, "Warmest regards, Laura San Giacomo." The day I finally brushed shoulders with Laura was up at the Universal City Walk, and we both did a double take, then turned toward each other and spontaneously embraced. I hadda ask her, "People always mistake me for you, but I've always wondered, does anyone ever mistake you for me?"

"I swear someone just told me they love my show, *The Nanny!*" she replied.

All in all, the third season seems like the best one yet. Dorothy has proved an outstanding director. Our numbers have skyrocketed and are way above our competitors'. This past week alone I got calls from Jon Feltheimer, Jeff Sagansky, *and* Les Moonves (our new CBS president), all congratulating me on our great numbers. Les said, "I love you, I love the show," to which I responded, "All right then, I'm hangin' up. That's all I needed to know!"

It's Friday, and I sit at my vanity in my trailer methodically fixing my hair and applying my makeup, for today is tape day. The phone rings. It's my mom calling to wish me luck on the show. "Oh, by the way, Cybill is copying you."

"Why, whaddya mean?" I reply.

"When her show goes to commercial, she says, 'We'll be

A bunch of us posed on the day we got our "Nanny" baseball caps. Unfortunately, our team never wins, but we enjoy playing. Not me, of course. I'm sleeping...

right back,' same as you." Can anyone be this naive? I wonder, when she tells me my sister's feeling much better. "It was a worm."

"A what?" I ask with incredulity.

"Remember I told ya she didn't feel good since Haiti?"

"Yeah."

"Well, it was a worm. They figured she must have eaten a rare hamburger or something, anyway, I guess the barium killed it, and when she went to go to the bathroom, a nine-inch worm came slidin' out!"

Well, if that wasn't the grossest thing I'd ever heard, and I'm groaning and gagging "Eww" when I hear my mother instructing my father to "Fast-forward, Morty, I don't like to see two women together, that don't turn me on." Do my ears deceive me?

"Ma, are you telling me you and Daddy were watching a porno film when *in-mitten-derrinin* [in the middle of it all] you decided to call and tell me about Nadine's worm?"

"Well, I thought you'd wanna know," she answered, and added, "your father wishes you good luck, too!"

We hung up and I tried to reach Howie on his private line,

but I dialed the wrong extension and accidentally got Danny Jacobson's office (he's the writer/executive producer of *Mad About You*). I said, "Who's this?"

He answered, "Who's *this*?"

"I asked you first."

"This is Danny Jacobson."

"Hi, Danny, it's Fran Drescher," to which he responded, "Fran, I was gonna call you to tell you I happened to catch your show with my wife Monday night and can understand why you're such a big hit. You're such a great comic, not afraid to throw yourself

Me and Uncle Miltie.

into it and just have fun. It must be a sheer pleasure to write for you, and I just wanted to let you know we think you're great!"

Wow, I thought. "Gee, Danny, this is the best wrong number I ever dialed, thanks!"

"Call me anytime," he added, and I said, "Well, now I've got ya number." I finished putting in my last curler and began to apply my makeup.

It just means so much when, unsolicited, people you respect in the industry enthusiastically praise the show and the work. It's a wonderful feeling to be so artistically and creatively satisfied. And when I look back at where we started, it's mind-blowing to think how far we've come. I'll tell ya, if there's one thing I've learned through all this it's that if you throw yourself into life, you always come back with gold (or at least a good idea or two).

I begin to run lines with Robbie while brushing on the blush. I recite my part, and Robbie reads all the other characters, each in his or her own voice, when Jay arrives with our lunch menu. On Fridays everything gets brought to me, including food, because on Fridays the whole day becomes about taping the show. First without an audience, then with one. As we go through the script there remain areas where jokes could stand improving, and even though it's tape day, we continue to rewrite all the way up until Dennis, our stage manager, yells, "That's a wrap."

Robbie calls Peter or Rob Sternin with the stuff I want to call attention to, and I slip into my shoes. Susan, our second stage manager, knocks on the door of my trailer and says that they're ready for me on the stage. As I enter the black hole, I leave outside the last bit of sunshine I will see of this day.

One time I told the phone page to call Robbie and tell him to walk the dog. Well, somehow the call went to Rob Sternin instead, but the same message was delivered.

Dear, sweet Rob Sternin, upon receiving the message that Fran wanted Rob to walk her dog, later admitted to thinking, "Hmmm, is Fran pulling a star trip? I mean, after all, I am the executive producer . . . but I shouldn't upset her on tape day . . . and I'm not really doing anything . . . I suppose I could walk the dog now and talk with Fran about it later . . . Okay, where's the leash?" he finally responded, and was actually in the parking lot walking Chester when Peter spotted him and asked what on earth he was doing, but knew as soon as Rob explained things that the message was meant for Robbie Schwartz, not Rob Sternin.

"Well, I was gonna say . . ." replied a relieved Rob Sternin as he handed Peter the leash and a tissue.

Backstage, the director and cast, arm in arm, stand in a circle and wish each other a great show, then we roar in unison, which signals Peter to start the intros. I come out last, raising my arms and running out from behind a screen to an audience of cheering fans.

I'll tell ya, over the many years in my career, as well as in my relationship with Peter, we've been poor and we've been rich, we've gone from agony to ecstasy, we've been to hell and back, and it's taught us to cherish life for all its simplicity as well as its grandeur. Listen, if I can do it, so can you. "GO and DO" is our motto, because ya never know! But I think the gal who was waxing my legs at the salon in the Tel Aviv Hilton said it best after I said to her, "Honey, you're killing me, why ya going so fast?"

"Life is so short, you must do everything fast if you want to get it all in!"

How profound, I thought, as I winced in pain.

"Meanwhile, doll, just finish my legs. I'll skip the bikini wax."

After the waxing I was asked to do an interview with one of the country's top journalists. I figured it would just be one of those run-of-the-mill pesky personality pieces. I was ushered into this fabulous office paneled in mahogany and burled wood, not at all what I was expecting. Suddenly the doors swing open and who walks in but the most gorgeous dead ringer for Omar Sharif in *Funny Girl*. I'll tell you, I could have broken into a chorus of "I Am Woman, You Are Man." He took my hand and kissed it. I giggled, and he looked at me with those deep brown eyes a little too deeply, practically a stare. I'll tell ya, I was beginning to feel a little uncomfortable. He turned on his tape recorder and started the interview, commenting on how lovely my perfume was, and how beautiful my body was, and is it getting warm in here? Then he slowly stood and walked closer. Oy, should I run out of here? Should I say something? Without warning he grabbed me and passionately pulled me toward him. He held my face and planted a hard, deep kiss on my . . . Only kidding! Got ya again.

Hey look, Ma. I made it.